Esther Price

Old Fashion

Candies

DAYTON ⟨⟩ CINCINNATI

Chocolate Covered Cherries

Esther Price's Memories

Chocolate Covered Cherries

Esther Price's Memories

Halstead & Meadows Publishing
Dayton, Ohio

Esther Price

and

Linda Otto Lipsett

Published in the United States of America by Halstead & Meadows Publishing.

All photographs collection of Esther Price.

Printed in the United States of America.

Title page: Esther Price packing chocolates for Red Cross project during World War II to send candy to the soldiers in the hospitals for Valentine's Day.

First Edition.

Library of Congress Cataloging-in-Publication Data

Price, Esther, 1904-
    Chocolate covered cherries : Esther Price's memories / Esther Price
and Linda Otto Lipsett.
        p.   cm.
    1. Price, Esther, 1904-   . 2. Women in business—United States-
-Biography. 3. Candy industry—United States—History.
I. Lipsett, Linda Otto, 1947- . II. Title.
HD9330.C652P75   1991
338.7'664153'092--dc20
[B]   91-42370
ISBN 0-9629399-1-9

Halstead & Meadows Publishing
Dayton, Ohio

In memory of my patient, loving husband, Ralph.

Acknowledgments

I want to thank all of my former employees from the bottom of my heart for sticking with me through thick and thin. More than not, I asked, "Can you stay a little longer?" And you usually did. I'm so grateful. Without your extra efforts, we could not have produced such a well-liked box of candy.

I also want to thank all of the people who made it possible for me to *stay* in business—all of the people who believed in me enough to loan me money.

Finally, I want to thank my family and their families for helping me. Early on, Esther Price Candies became a family business with my son and daughters, sons-in-law, daughter-in-law, and later their children and their husbands all working for me. I want to especially thank my sister and her husband for bringing in that Guernsey cream each day and for helping me when they could.

If you think you can do something with all of your heart, nothing is impossible. And all of you helped me make that dream come true.

Esther Price
Dayton, Ohio
October, 1991

This book has been written from recorded tapes, many hours of telephone conversations between Los Angeles and Dayton, hand-written additions by Esther, as well as many days working side-by-side editing the manuscript.

For their insightful contributions to this book, we would like to express our deepest thanks to Helena Tartar and Johnnie Crutcher. Also, the memories of family members have been invaluable, adding so much to this book. Our thanks to Jack and Ann Price, Evelyn Price Freese, Bill Otto, and William Otto.

Finally, there is one person who did more than anyone else to make this book possible—Eileen Price Kelley recorded the many hours of tapes that form the backbone of the book. At all times she was an integral part of the tapings, always attempting to jog her mother's memories.

Linda Otto Lipsett

Esther Price

October, 1991

Esther

Contents

Introduction

There are pictures of women's faces in frames in candy-store windows across America—Fanny Farmer, Mary See.... For the most part those women are forgotten; today only their names remain as company names and the names on boxes of candy. Perhaps, in many ways those women's stories are similar. They began their candymaking in their kitchens desperately working during difficult times to make some money for their families in a man's working world.

One such woman is Esther Price, the founder of Esther Price Candies of Dayton, Ohio. She began making candy to help make ends meet during the Depression, fighting every step of the way against all odds to *continue* making candy. Always she had to hold fast to her unyielding determination and to her deep-seated belief that nothing is impossible. Then after fifty years of great success, she sold the business in 1976. Like many of those other candymakers, the name "Esther Price" of Esther Price Candies has become a company name synonymous with the candy. "Have an Esther Price," they say, meaning, "Have a piece of candy." Soon, if not already by younger generations, Esther Price, the woman with the dream and determination, would be forgotten, too. Instead, she is here to tell her story. Esther Price was a great candymaker and given a kettle and the ingredients, I know she still is a great candymaker—a true candymaker at heart—forever. And that's the story *she* tells.

I have a different one to tell, for Esther Price is my grandmother—I am her first grandchild. Grandma tells a story of working day and night making candy, but somehow she managed to do so much more. She is the "Santa Claus" of my life, always there for me. It was always so exciting when Grandma arrived, usually late in the evening. She always had surprises. Chocolates, of course, but many times she brought a new frilly lace dress for my concert that week, something special to eat, caramel for a sore throat. Best of all, she brought an exuberance for life, boundless energy, laughter and love.

As a little girl in church on Sunday mornings, I'd lie in her lap. I remember her hands then. They were rough and deeply etched in a myriad of fine brown lines—stains from chocolate. In fact, they even smelled faintly like chocolate. I loved her hands stroking my head, holding my hand. They *were* Grandma. Later in the day, my report with pictures due the next day, we'd go to Grandma's house. She would take me down the steps of the old house into the basement, where she had a little, or a lot, of everything. She never failed to find what I needed. And there was always warmth, happiness, and good things to eat at Grandma's. There was even an aroma in her house (in every house she lived in) that was truly Grandma's alone. The perfect blend of oatmeal cookies baking and a rump roast in the oven? No, it had to be more than that. It had to be touched by Grandma. It was a delicious, indescribable smell—it *was* Grandma.

She always made Christmas and Easter special days of the year. We grandchildren never knew how exhausted she was. Nevertheless, Christmas afternoon or evening we anxiously went to Grandma's to see what Santa had left. There was always a real spruce tree lit up sparkling with icicles, special presents for each one of us under it. And there were always good things to eat. That was a given at Grandma's. She was a *great* cook.

On Easter, I remember all of us grandchildren waiting in the house while the Easter Bunny finished hiding baskets in the yard. Grandma *filled* Easter baskets and the large cartons she used for packing candy with Easter eggs of every variety that she herself had shaped, that Grandpa had hand decorated. And there were pans of caramel, bags of foil eggs, jelly beans, nuts, and usually a large, stuffed animal. Then the Easter Bunny hid them in the huge yard surrounding the candy factory and the house. We'd crawl through our secret hiding places made by branches of huge, old gnarled bushes to find our own sack of silver—there were seven hidden, one for each grandchild. Each bag held a different amount of change, but usually about twenty dollars. There were the baby ducks one year, baby rabbits in the yard in boxes another, even black French poodles one year.

Grandma was magical, a party in herself on our vacations at her cottage at Bear Lake. Always, Grandma was the center, the focus of fun. And she taught many of her grandchildren to swim. "Just lay out and move your arms back and forth," she'd say, helping to hold us up. Little did we know that she did not know how to swim.

"Never put tomato in your iron skillet," she called out as I was leaving for my new married life. *That's my grandma.*

Always I remember her being there to give advice, to direct, to help, but most of all to teach me by showing love, generosity, and the joy of giving.

I love you, Grandma.
And thanks for sharing your special memories.
I consider this my greatest gift from you.

Linda Otto Lipsett

October 1, 1991

Authors of this book, Esther and Linda, in front of Fauver Avenue candy-store window, 1948.

"Dover Street house, just up the street from Schiller School, where I first learned to make fudge. Maude, Paul, Mama, and I are standing on the front porch. Dad is sitting on the banister."

Chapter One

Oh, Mother! I learned how to make fudge.

I was born on March 6, 1904, in Hamilton, Ohio, across the street from a papermill and was named Esther Rose Rohman. My middle name was after my dad's father's mother. My sister, born seventeen months earlier, had been named Maude Ella after my mother. I was a premature baby of seven months born with dark blue, shriveled skin and no fingernails or toenails. I was so frail that they didn't know if I'd take my next breath. Everybody told my parents I couldn't live. From then on, my Dad was constantly looking for someone to help me.

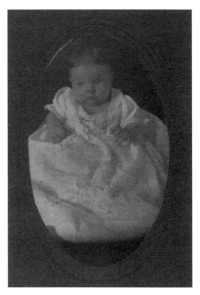

Esther at four months of age.

My father learned toolmaking from his father, and one month after my birth, he got employment at the National Cash Register Company in Dayton. We moved to Dayton into a few rooms on Park Street and were there a short time when my parents bought a house a few miles north at the corner of Dover and Wyoming Street. My father bought the house directly from the owners, who were able to accept the monthly payment that he could afford. There was a chicken coup with Plymouth Rock chickens, pigeons, and rabbits in the back yard. A traction car passed one hundred yards from the front door. A school of eight grades was about a mile down the hill from our back door.

I was still in poor health when I was three years old. I had an older brother, Paul, and a sister, Maude. Mama was expecting another baby. Dad met a man that told him about an Indian that could mix up a brew that would heal me. He told me he was going to bring the man home, but I never dreamed he'd be a real Indian fully dressed in feathers. Dad opened up the outside doors and took me by the wrist down into the cool cellar. (He always held me by the wrist. He never held my hand. Years later when he took me on the back end of the trolley when I felt sick, he took me by the wrist.) The Indian followed us in. Oh, I was so scared of that Indian—his feathers and all. I had never seen anything like that. And then to go down into the basement and meet him—I felt like something had me.

First he put both hands on my head and shoulders and powwowed over me (prayer in his sight). Then he mixed up a brew out of herbs and said I had to take a tablespoon before every meal. It wasn't that bad—it tasted like something I really wanted, like something I really needed. I started getting better right away. I have no idea what it was—it was his secret for helping somebody when they were sick. He showed Dad how to make it, and I can see a little granite bucket about so big around. It couldn't be aluminum. He told me not to miss taking it. For at least a year I was taken to the basement before each meal, and I swallowed my tablespoon of brew. I seemed to get stronger all the time and started running around and playing with the other children. And finally I could eat. My appetite had been so very, very poor, but the potion gave me a good appetite—evidently for sugar because I surely wanted sugar all the time after that. A piece of candy always thrilled me.

"Grandma always sat in a rocker preparing her vegetables underneath these trees right behind the grocery store. I am holding my cousin, whom I was allowed to push in the carriage all around the neighborhood."

After school it seems as though we would play a game to see who got home the fastest. I was lucky because right next door we had German neighbors with six babies. Usually one of the babies was awake so I could take it for a ride. I went up to the door and the minute they saw me, they would say the baby was asleep yet or they'd have it ready in a minute or so. From the time that I could push a carriage (I don't think I was much over seven—I know the baby buggy was bigger than I was), I would take any baby that was awake for a ride and go to the bakeshop to get bread for the neighbors after school. I always acted as if they were my doll babies; I just loved to hold them and take care of them.

Ellen Burcky Augspurger, Esther's grandmother.   Ella Augspurger Rohman, Esther's mother.

"At the side of the Augspurger home in West Middletown, Ohio, c. 1897. Building to the left is where they brought in the milk after milking. Left to right, Aunt Carrie, Aunt Elizabeth, Grandpa Augspurger, Aunt Anna, Mother, Aunt Amelia."

Wedding photgraph of Ella A.
Augspurger and John J. Rohman,
Esther's mother and father, 1899.

"On Dover Street, Dad with his new
Harley-Davidson. Rabbit hutch in
the rear. Left to right, Mama, Edgar,
Esther, Maude, Paul, and Dad."

A lady stopped me one day and asked if I would take care of her nine-month-old son after school until 5:30 p.m. I was pleased. Now I wouldn't have to search for a baby that was awake. At the end of the week I received a half dollar. With that money and my pennies, I thought it would only be a short time until I could buy a baby of my very own.

Then one day Mother said the doctor was bringing another baby to the German lady. I sat on my front steps to meet him—I thought I might have a baby all my own. Mother would call me to do something for her, and I rushed to get it done and got right back out on the steps waiting for the doctor again, but somehow or other I missed him.

We played baseball. We went to the back of the house and south a block, and there was a big empty commons where the boys met—everybody met to play baseball. And I did love to play baseball. I thought I was pretty good. We got away from the table right away; we didn't sit. I was supposed to be doing dishes, and when I'd see Mama coming after me, I'd run the other way and be in the house doing dishes before she got back. We played jump rope and jacks and different things like that, too.

When I was eight or nine, Mama made me my first good dress. It was white, and all the way down the front and around the square neck was lace with blue ribbon woven through. Mama made a bow with ribbons hanging down. I can remember being so proud and happy. Then one day Mama wanted to take us to church. She belonged to the Mennonite church way down on Xenia Avenue. I wore my new dress, and somebody really growled. Their faith forbade anything fancy, and I had ribbons and lace all over my dress. Mama was so embarrassed because of how people stared at my dress.

"This is the flower circle where Maude (on the right) and I sat every Sunday afternoon waiting for Mom and Dad while they visited Great-grandfather Mueller. He had lost his leg in the Civil War."

Edgar, Maude, and I all slept on the same bed. My older brother, Paul, had his own bed upstairs. Right in between the two bedrooms was an opening to go upstairs. Whenever we got too noisy and didn't go to sleep, Mama would put on her false face, shake the curtain, and go, "Whoo, hoo, hoo, hoo, hoo, hoo." We'd see that false face, and we'd jump under the covers and never say a word the rest of the night.

Every Saturday night Mama rolled up my hair on long, kid curlers and made long curls for our Sunday trip to the Soldier's Home. My dad and mom visited my great-grandfather Mueller, who had lost his leg in the Civil War. On Dover Street, Mama had a smaller-size, regular stove. She'd open the oven door, put the laundry tub in front of it, and give us a bath.

"I played with dolls until I was allowed to take care of real babies. The traction lines are in the street."

Mama was sick and Grandma (Dad's mother) came to stay and help. Grandma was really strict. It seems we were old enough to want our own things. We had the habit of hanging our clothes on the dresser-drawer knobs, and she said we "dassn't" do that; they had to be hung in the closets. She'd complain to Dad, and Dad would give us a beating for doing that. We wanted to go to Sunday school, but she wouldn't let us have any pennies because we "dassn't" give our daddy's hard-earned money to that man.

Dad used to go hunting on the Kinsinger's farm, and their daughter Esther let me hold her big, beautiful doll. I'll never forget that. I didn't have any doll at that time and was really too small to hold her big, beautiful doll, but I took good care of it. I wanted that doll so bad. I probably wasn't old enough for a doll when I got mine. My parents kept saying Santa Claus was going to bring Maude a doll and next year he would bring me one, but I wanted a doll that year. At the last second they realized it wasn't going to work without my having a doll, too. They went downtown and bought a doll, but it only had underwear on it. Later Mama made clothes for it.

Sunday afternoon was the only time Dad was off work, and that's when he would make different things to eat. From the time we kids were tiny, for Sunday afternoon Dad made popcorn and a little tray of butterscotch candy, and we always had apples. He greased the platter, poured the candy on it, and let it cool. Then he would pick up the butterscotch in his hand and slap the back of the knife against it. It would break into pieces, and we were each allowed to have one piece of it. But we had to suck it. We weren't allowed to chew it—if Dad heard us crunching it, he'd give us the dickens.

In the beginning of the winter, Dad would always buy a bushel of potatoes and apples. Beneath the basement steps was a place that was still dirt. He dug that up and put carrots and red beets down there. That way we had carrots and red beets all winter, whenever we wanted them.

I can remember the first day that Dad bought a car. He bought one of the very first cars that was made. It was called "Apple 8." I can remember him parking that car in front of the curb and telling us to come and look at it. From then on, we could drive to Cincinnati and back and visit his father and mother at the Empire Grocery Store. There were no paved streets then. They were all gravel roads. All of us kids would sit in the back seat of the car. At that time there were no windows to roll up; there were only transparent curtains that snapped into place, and you had to put them in from the outside when the car was stopped. So we only used them when it was raining or very cold. When Dad drove, he chewed tobacco. Everytime he spit out the window, his tobacco juice sprayed us in the back seat.

We mostly drove when the weather was decent. It was a long trip because there

"At the back of the grocery store. We are leaving for home in Dad's Apple 8."

were no short cuts. It was almost a day's trip one way so we would stay overnight at the grocery store. Then we had to start home early enough so that we could make it all the way. There was a railroad crossing up a steep grade immediately to the left of the grocery. You couldn't see if a train was coming until you got up the hill. Those old cars would stall as they tried to slow down to see if a train was coming. Grandma was the grocery person; she ran the grocery-store business, not Grandpa. In the grocery-store business, the women always took over; the men had to go out to work. There wasn't that much money in the food business, but you did have food for your own family that way. You always had vegetables that had to be used, and fruit that had to be used..... Grandma had the store from the time her children were little. At that time she only sold vegetables and fruits. She didn't make things for the store then—she had four small children. Grandpa went out and did toolmaking.

I went to Schiller School down the hill just a few blocks from the house. As long as I can remember, I couldn't wait until the seventh grade when I would have my home-economics class and have sewing and cooking. How I loved it. One week was sewing and one was cooking. I made a dress that I continued to wear long after I was out of school. We had a cooking class near Christmas. We had our own little hot plate (two girls shared a two-burner hot plate, one girl on each end of it). The teacher told us that we were going to make candy and taught us how to make fudge so that we could make fudge for our mothers for Christmas. When we got all through making the fudge and dividing it between the two girls, there didn't seem to be but a couple of pieces left, and she told us, "Now take this home to your mother for Christmas." So I ran all the way up the street, and I was nibbling on the candy, too. I can remember Mama always at the side door waiting for us to come up the street. Everyday we ran. We just acted as if we couldn't wait to get home because we always had something to tell her that we did at school. That day I said, "Oh, Mother! Oh, Mother! I learned how to make fudge. Here's a piece of it. Here's a taste of it. Can I make some right now?" Not waiting for an answer, I scrambled to the kitchen, got the pan out, and stirred up sugar, cocoa, milk, and a pinch of salt as I remembered from school. The fudge didn't last but a few minutes after I made it. I was so inspired with the results that I wanted to keep on cooking another batch. From then on we thought nothing about it—when anyone was coming, I made fudge. At that time I think I only used about one cup of sugar and a little over a half cup of milk. It was just a little, tiny batch and didn't take long to cook. (Later on, I changed the cocoa to the kind I like so well—to Nestles. In fact, I think I had tried it in the cocoa I made to drink and liked it so much.)

To save every penny Mother walked miles to any grocery that had a sale. The

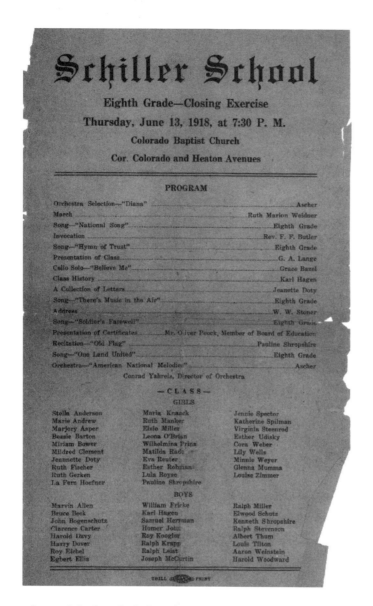

Schiller School

Eighth Grade—Closing Exercise
Thursday, June 13, 1918, at 7:30 P. M.
Colorado Baptist Church
Cor. Colorado and Heaton Avenues

PROGRAM

Orchestra Selection—"Diana" .... Ascher
March .... Ruth Marion Weidner
Song—"National Song" .... Eighth Grade
Invocation .... Rev. F. F. Butler
Song—"Hymn of Trust" .... Eighth Grade
Presentation of Class .... G. A. Lange
Cello Solo—"Believe Me" .... Grace Bazel
Class History .... Karl Hagen
A Collection of Letters .... Jeanette Doty
Song—"There's Music in the Air" .... Eighth Grade
Address .... W. W. Stoner
Song—"Soldier's Farewell" .... Eighth Grade
Presentation of Certificates .... Mr. Oliver Poock, Member of Board of Education
Recitation—"Old Flag" .... Pauline Shropshire
Song—"One Land United" .... Eighth Grade
Orchestra—"American National Melodies" .... Ascher

Conrad Yahrels, Director of Orchestra

—CLASS—
GIRLS

Stella Anderson	Maria Knaack	Jennie Spector
Marie Andrew	Ruth Manker	Katherine Spilman
Marjory Asper	Elsie Miller	Virginia Steenrod
Bessie Barton	Leona O'Brian	Esther Udisky
Miriam Bower	Wilhelmina Prinz	Cora Weber
Mildred Clement	Matilda Rade	Lily Wells
Jeannette Doty	Eva Reuter	Minnie Weyer
Ruth Fischer	Esther Rohman	Glenna Mumma
Ruth Gerken	Lula Royse	Louise Zimmer
La Fern Hoefner	Pauline Shropshire	

BOYS

Marvin Allen	William Fricke	Ralph Miller
Bruce Beck	Karl Hagen	Elwood Schutz
John Bogenschutz	Samuel Herrman	Kenneth Shropshire
Clarence Carter	Homer John	Ralph Stevenson
Harold Davy	Roy Koogler	Albert Thum
Harry Dover	Ralph Krapp	Louis Tilton
Roy Eichel	Ralph Leist	Aaron Weinstein
Egbert Ellis	Joseph McCurtin	Harold Woodward

TOILL PRINT

Having learned to make her first fudge in school, Esther was well on her way to becoming a candymaker upon her eighth-grade graduation from Schiller School. (See "Esther Rohman" listed in middle column.)

minute Mother left for the store, I was tempted to make more fudge. My sister was with me, and I thought if we ate every crumb and washed the dishes and even opened the doors to get the smell out, nothing would be said. But the minute Mother opened the door, she said, "You made more candy." We wondered how on earth she knew and felt very selfish that we hadn't even saved her a piece. The next Saturday it was time for Mother to walk miles and climb a steep hill with a basket of groceries to save a few cents, but I was possessed to make more candy. I had been given a small bottle of perfume, and I thought I would pour it around the kitchen. Then no one could smell the candy. I made the candy, and Maude and I ate it all right away, did the dishes, and opened the doors. Then I put out some of the perfume in the kitchen—I just took the bottle and splashed it here and there in the corners of the room. I thought for sure now Mama couldn't tell that I made candy. But the minute that she opened the door, she knew. This time we were warned never to make any more candy, not even for company. She asked us to promise that we wouldn't make it anymore. I was so disturbed—it seemed that making fudge was a part of me. Maude was always at my side. We both stuffed the candy and did the dishes as quickly as we could because it seemed that sometimes Mama got back from the grocery store so much sooner than we expected.

Esther at age 14

Then I didn't make candy for a long time. Candy wasn't even mentioned, and Mother never went that distance for the groceries. Then one day she had a sale to go to, and my thoughts deceived me again. I was determined to make more candy. This time I had a new plan. I had heard someone say that they burned their potatoes, and so that their husband couldn't tell, they burned a string. The string covered the odor. So when Mama went to the sale, I made more candy. I cleaned up everything, and then I got a string. Inside the register in the living room was a metal box, and I laid that string in the metal box and lit a match to it. It burned and, oh, what a smell, but Mama surely wouldn't smell the candy this time. The second Mother came home, she yelled, "The house is on fire! The house is on fire!" She went into such a rage and ran to find the fire. I told her what I had done. She grabbed me and I got a spanking I never forgot, nor did I ever make candy and try to cover it up again. I could have burned the house down, she said.

I don't remember sneaking to make candy again after that. After three tries I realized there just was no way that I could hide that candymaking. After that, I asked Mama if I could make some candy for company. When we had an evening that we didn't have anything to do, she'd let me make candy.

Many times Mama broke the yardstick over me. One time I asked to go to my friend Margaret Barnes's next door. We were going to play cards. Her parents weren't home. Margaret was a little older, and she always had lots of friends. Anyway, she never said anything about boys being there; she just told me to come over and play cards so I went over. Margaret didn't have the curtains all drawn and Mama could see the boys inside. She came to the front door with the yardstick in her hand and broke it over me. Then she told me to get home, that I had no business over there without their mother and dad home. I was so embarrassed. I felt I was grown up and didn't think I needed to have that.

From the time I was about five or six years old, my sister, Maude, and I would take turns spending a month in the summer at Grandma's grocery store that belonged to my dad's mother, father, older sister, and brother. It was in Hartwell, Ohio, just north of Cincinnati. The rest of the summer we spent at Mother's sister Aunt Emmy's farm in the country in West Middletown, Ohio. There we got up early in the morning and were in the strawberry patch by daybreak. Mother's father, Grandpa Augspurger, lived right up the road. I loved to watch him slop the pigs. Grandpa always brought milk back to what he called the "slop house," and he poured some into the bucket for the cats and the dogs. Then he poured some out for the pigs. He had some large crocks lined up and he poured the rest into the crocks. He let the milk set until the cream settled on top. Then the women dipped off the cream that they wanted for the table and the cooking and put the rest into the milk.

We weren't home at all in the summer because Mama had a tiny yard with the traction car going right past the door—it actually shook the windows in the house as it did when the train went by. Actually, the traction lines were in the street and it seems that it shook the street. So we spent most of the summer away, either at the grocery store or at the farm.

The Empire Grocery Store was built aside a railroad track that angled as though the train was coming through the middle of the house. When the train blew its whistle for the station that was directly across the street, we would run through the store and to an upstairs window that shook and rattled as if it were falling out. We would stand there and watch the train, feeling safe that we were inside.

I met Ralph Price when I was very young. His family lived several blocks down the street from my grandma's grocery store. He was from a family of nine. Ralph was not over nine or ten when he started working there—he was just old enough to run small errands. It is difficult to say when he earned his first fifty cents because there was no age limit on how old you had to be to do errands. He waited on customers

"At Aunt Emmy's farm on my summer vacation. I would say this was my first blouse and skirt. I was quite dressed up. Before that I always wore school dresses."

and filled the vinegar jars, did all the odd jobs, swept the leaves. The first year that I can remember, he drove the horse and wagon. The next year they got a truck. He only took Maude on his deliveries the first year. Later, Ralph would take whichever one of us was there on his delivery truck. When we were older, once a week Ralph would take Maude or me to the show or to Chester Park.

Right out in front of the store was a big circle, and it had a great big fountain in the middle of it. The horses would be lined up there, drinking. Then they would go on to wherever they had to go. Across the street and straight in front was the train station. One time a young man tried to jump the train and missed it and got both legs cut off. We didn't go over there and see him because there was a crowd, but I can remember what a commotion that was.

As people came in the big, wide grocery-store door, to the right were all the vegetables and fruits; to the left, the big, long candy case. The thing I liked the best was filling the candy case. I just went crazy to fill up the candy case and make all the dishes look perfect with the pieces of candy stacked as high as I could stack them. It was all wrapped penny candy bought in five-pound boxes. Aunt Mary said the reason I wanted to fix the candy case was so that I could eat all I wanted, but I didn't eat it because I knew what they were thinking. I just loved filling the candy case. You know what a job that was—every piece on the plates just so, and the next row just so. Then everytime they sold some, I'd have to fill it in and straighten it up. They sold a lot of that penny candy. The customers would buy ten-to-fifteen-cents worth of what they called "sucking candy." And when customers paid their bills, Grandma gave them a small sack of candy.

At the rear of the store were large cooler cases for sandwich meat, cheese, milk, and so on. In the family kitchen joining the store were two large lard cans, a ham in each simmering all night in water, brown sugar, mustard, a cup of vinegar, and salt and pepper. In the morning before breakfast, they'd take the ham out, lay it on a tray, and let it cool down gradually. Then we could first get our breakfast. About eleven o'clock, they would slice the ham by hand as thin as they could slice it, and sandwiches were made to sell. You never tasted anything so good in your life; it was so tender and tasty. The sales kept growing and Grandma kept cooking more ham. You can't believe the work. That was a constant, everyday thing to do. But, oh my, people would come from all over to get those ham sandwiches. The demand was so great that as soon as the evening meal was prepared, Grandma and Aunt Mary had to put the lard cans back onto the stove to simmer more hams all night for the next day.

Behind the meat case was a storage room with empty barrels and kegs of every kind of vinegar, where customers would bring their gallon jugs and have them filled with a vinegar of their choice. When Ralph was near, that was his responsibility.

Uncle Walter went to market every morning at four o'clock and got fresh vegetables. Grandma sorted the bananas every day. We had to eat the bananas that were ripe, the ones that were going to spoil. She went over the lettuce every day, all the vegetables, too. What needed to be used, she cooked. As soon as the evening meal was over, the family met in the stockroom behind the meat case where empty wooden barrels were waiting to be filled with the ripe vegetables of the season. On Sunday afternoons, instead of having card parties, we would have a pickling party or a canning party or a sauerkraut party. Family and friends would meet in this storage room. We never made more than one thing in a day. We would all make sauerkraut or we would all make pickles.... It was get-together time to make barrels of sauerkraut, pickles, or schnibble beans (they were cut longer and cut diagonally; some were pickled and some were plain). For the sauerkraut one person would wash the heads of the cabbage, another one would cut them in half, another would be running them on the grater. They always worked as a team stomping

"Grandma Rohman with four of her grandchildren (Edgar, Maude, Paul, Esther) at the side of the Empire Grocery Store. The grape arbors are in the rear."

them down in a big barrel, as if you had a big potato masher. We worked to fill the wooden barrels until late in the evening, just stopping to grab a sandwich. Then we kept right on working. One could call it a production party, where you could see what was accomplished.

"Back porch of Grandma's first grocery store. Front row, left to right, Grandma (Rose Mueller) Rohman, ___ Riddle, Aunt Mary, ___ Riddle. Back row, Peter Rohman, ___ Riddle, Walter Rohman (Peter Rohman's son), ___ Riddle."

We did every kind of pickles. Mostly we just washed the pickles (small cucumbers were called pickles). Some of them we would cut thin, some we would cut in half, and some in quarters. It would be according to what kind of pickle we were making. But we always had a big glass jar with a wide, open mouth full of pickles.

They made all of their food. They made it for themselves and to sell. Later on, after Grandma died, Aunt Mary built a great big, long room that went on out from the store the full length of the grape arbor; it went way back and angled out close to the railroad track. We called it the "Betty Kramer Kitchen"—I don't know where she got that name—I never heard her say—but it was probably a jelly that she liked, and she called it by that name. She made every kind of jelly. Everything had to be fresh fruit of the season, and it was so good. You can't find any jelly on the shelf like that now. I don't know how she made it so that it didn't taste too cooked—it tasted more like fresh fruit. I wanted to eat the whole jar. Aunt Mary worked constantly. In fact, the women never did anything but work. In other words, they never sat down; they just put one thing on or another.

Down at the grocery store, Aunt Mary used the Ouija Board when she soaked her feet, but she couldn't understand why it wouldn't work—it just flew from one side to the other. Finally, it slowed up enough so she could read, "MARY, TAKE YOUR FEET OUT OF WATER. WATER IS A NON CONDUCTOR." Grandma used the Ouija Board, too. Later, Mary gave it to me. Years later when it spelled out that a relative with TB was going to die, I felt it was something evil and threw it into the coal furnace.

"The peace of being in the country with the wonderful fresh air and then the surprise of Ralph coming to visit me....

I'm in my gray vest and knicker set and I bought the hat to go with it."

Chapter Two

Esther-O, I love you.

When Ralph was eighteen, his mother died during the 1918 flu epidemic. Aunt Mary Rohman and Grandma gave Ralph a room at the grocery store and took care of him. That was his only home from the time I was fourteen. So from then on, he was always at the grocery store. His mother left a six-month-old baby (Paul), who was given to his dad's sister, Aunt Mary Patton. Ralph's family was completely broken up. All of the children lived with different relatives.

In a room behind the meat case at the grocery store were all the pickle barrels, sauerkraut barrels, and barrels of vinegar of every kind. People would bring in their gallon jugs to be filled. That was usually Ralph's chore. One day I was standing close to the door when a customer handed his gallon jug to Ralph to fill. Ralph asked me to go along. And I did. While the vinegar was dripping slowly into the small opening of that gallon jug, he grabbed me and kissed me. I was shocked. My face turned fiery red. When we came out with the gallon of vinegar, everyone laughed at my red face. I raced upstairs to my bedroom and cried myself to sleep. I felt that all our families were close and we always kissed hello and good-bye; I couldn't understand how this kiss could be so much different. How could this kiss make the sparks fly?

"Just prior to her death, Ralph's mother (Emma Powell Price) holding her youngest son, Paul; her son Bob standing."

I felt like my whole body had been electrocuted or something. Oh my, I'll never forget that. I was thrilled but scared that I had done something wrong. I was sure I would have a baby, but I didn't know how you got a baby. Mama always said the doctor brought all those babies the German lady had next door.

When I was fifteen, I went on my vacation to Grandma's grocery store, but I could only stay a couple of weeks—Margaret Barnes's mother had asked me to go to Indian Lake with them on their vacation. When I left the grocery store, I didn't act like there was anything different and, oh, I was happy to be going on my vacation with Margaret. But Ralph seemed a little more concerned about my leaving this time. I got a letter from him in three days at Margaret's vacation spot saying how much he missed me and could we write each other. He didn't say anything about liking me; he just asked if he could write to me. I was so surprised to get that letter.

Hartwell

Nov. 9.

Dearest Friend:

  Perhaps you will have some difficulty in deciphering this Esther but I'm trying hard to make it legible. Am writing with a pad resting on my knee by the fire in the parlor. Very nice here and cozy but I'm all alone and – lonesome.

  Mary, Frank and I went to the Palace last night; saw a fine show. Say, honey, just ate an apple (never was fond of them till I started counting seeds; queer isn't it,) and there was nine. Was very careful too to count them all. Have had three, four and nine so far. Tells volumes doesn't it? And in a way, perhaps, better than I could myself. I had a letter today from my kid brother; he said he met a young lady up there and has been out several times with her and that she is the most beautiful girl in the world. While I love my brother very much and respect his judgment in many things I told him I couldn't agree with him in that one respect. Told him I had the pleasure of meeting two girls this summer that could outshine his forty ways. He and I are going to wage a verbal battle from now on I think for he resents any attempt to dispute his word.

  Well dear are you bored by this yet or maybe you haven't been able to read it at all. Bye till Sunday Esther. I, too, hope we have a nice day this sunday. The last few have been fine so far as weather is concerned, but I'd rather work than put in many days as I have my Sundays.

  Love & x's.

Then it was my sister's time to spend at Grandma's, and she would accompany Ralph in the truck as he delivered groceries to all the customers who had called in for orders. When her vacation was over, Maude asked Ralph to write her, and he did.

One Sunday the relatives from the grocery store came to visit us. Mama said, "Now when I call for help in the kitchen, Esther, I want you to come because Ralph is coming to see Maude. She is closer to his age." No problem. I loved to do dishes when I had plenty of good soap suds and hot water. Then we just sat on the swing on the front porch. I sat on one side of Ralph, and Maude sat on the other. No matter where we went, we sat on each side of him. All the way through, Ralph was like family, and he treated us like family. I don't think I felt I loved Ralph then. He was always Maude's, and I never even thought of him in the way of a boyfriend—for at least three years anyway. Time flew by and letters kept coming.

I had learned to dance at the barn dance on Saturday nights. We just got out and danced and swung around with anybody that would swing us around, and then, of course, a lot of the people were relation. Dad drove us down to the country in the Apple 8 for the barn dance. All I remember is that everybody gathered and sang and danced. Dad loved anything that was a gathering together with singing and dancing. And I don't think Mama hated it because she gathered with everybody else—but she *never* danced.

When I was about fifteen, we danced at Island Park. They had a beautiful dance hall. The dances were advertised, and Maude and I got to go. We went one night a week. We had a certain time we had to be home. We'd take the streetcar (we lived only four doors up the street from where you got off the streetcar). I learned from just getting out there and dancing; I just swayed with the music. I thought it was a disaster if I missed a dance. Oh, I was just not liked if I missed a dance. If I didn't have every dance booked up from the very start, I just thought I was no good. Maude would be sitting back feeling sad because she didn't have every dance booked up. I sat there, and the boys just kept coming up to me and asking me for whichever dance I had open—the first dance, fifth.... I had every dance every time. When Maude and I started to go with Ralph, he said he hated to say it, but he sure was thinking a lot about me going to those dances. You couldn't get him to dance. I remember one night I put my arms around him and tried to get him to dance, and he pulled away. He didn't like that. He didn't even want to see me dance. In his letters he wrote how he worried when I said that I was going to the dance. That upset him terribly.

Not too long after that, there was a shooting at the park over girlfriends. I don't ever remember going back again.

"I was sixteen. I had the dress made. It was a very beautiful, lime-green dress and one of my favorite. I wore it for my graduation from the school in salesmanship."

Hartwell
Nov. 15.

Dear Esther:

Well here it is Thursday of another week and no letter. But you're excused as I know you must have had a good and sufficient reason for not writing. Come to think of it I believe you said your dance was scheduled for Tuesday. Am I right? I wonder if you will be surprised to receive your Saturday letter as usual. I just finished delivering a few minutes ago and am in the store alone now. Have to be out late tonight so I must write now. It has been midnight for me every night this week. Isn't that terrible? But Friday and Saturday I intend to make up for lost sleep. And then too, I can stay in all day Sunday.

There is nothing in the way of news this time; nothing ever happens here but the same old routine day after day. Oh yes, Frank mentioned the position with Wholesale again. Rather, I brought the subject up myself and his opinion is still favorable. Speed the day. I firmly feel in my own mind that I can handle it and only want the opportunity to prove that I can. This is some scratching but the best I can do under the circumstances.

Grandpa Rohman is feeling better again; he went to work yesterday. Everybody else is all well.

I've had no less than half a dozen people tell me this week that I'm getting fat. The scales fail to prove it, have gained only four pounds.

Do you remember Esther when you was down here on your vacation and John Waldman came in for vinegar? You and I went in the back room after it and we stayed a bit longer than he thought we should. Well, he never sees me now but what he mentions that incident. I think you will remember it. I never forget things like that. And this morning I waited on him for a gallon of cider. The keg was just about empty and it took me quite a while to get it. He said, "Ralph, you should have that keg in the back room, then you wouldn't care how long it took." I said, "No, I'd rather have it here, there is no one here I'd want to go with me." Forgive me for bringing up old recollections but I just thought I'd tell you about it. Excuse writing and answer soon.

your friend always

Ralph

It was time for another vacation at the grocery store. Aunt Mary had a player piano. It had a large bench with a back on it. In the evenings Ralph and I would sit side-by-side playing the player piano. One song Ralph chose was,

Molly-O, I love you.
Tis yourself knows it's true.

But instead of "Molly-O," he sang,

Esther-O, I love you.
Tis yourself knows it's true.

Then he grabbed me and kissed me. The embrace was so great that we broke the back off the bench. It was so embarrassing and I was scared to tell Grandma, and that seemed to be the last I saw Ralph on that vacation. I kept repeating to myself,

"Ralph's lodge picture at age twenty, the first picture he gave me."

"Esther-O, I love you. Tis yourself knows it's true." But I didn't know it was true.

Vacation days were over and I left for home and school. Little did I think that would be my last time at Grandma's because I was working at school on my lunch hour waiting on teachers and then running most of the way downtown to McCrory's ten-cent store after school. I had a job making Neapolitan ice-cream bars. (I wasn't quite sixteen, but if you looked as if you were able to fill the job, nobody in those days really bothered about how old you were.) I wouldn't get a vacation until I had worked there one year, and then it would be only one week. Then I got a job in a dress department at Rike Kumler Department Store and didn't have any vacation coming for another year. I didn't see Ralph for a long time. All we did was write letters. Ralph wrote me at Rike Kumler Company and Maude at the house on Highland Avenue. He said his letters to me were too personal for the whole family to see because he said many times, "I love you, I love you, I love

Dear Esther:

This morning I received quite the nicest surprise I've had for some time — your letter. Nothing could be sweeter but you in person. And the pictures aren't half bad are they? I do wish though I could have had the one I was on with the "sin twisters." Everyone thought they were fine. I didn't realize that Maude took so to heart, the little argument as to the position each of you should take in that one picture. But the expression on her face seems that she did. It isn't natural — not at all like Maudie. I am real anxious now to see how the others will be. There is one in particular I hope will be good, don't you?

I have some encouraging news this time, Esther. Grandma is getting better and stronger each day. She sat up in bed for about ten minutes today. She said to send her regards to all and that she is glad you like your new position. Also to say that they wouldn't write if I was going to. It would have to be some thing very serious or important that would keep me from answering your letters.

More good news — to me at least. My vacation starts Saturday and if nothing prevents am going to take three weeks. Will go to Wellston and I don't expect to do a thing but eat, sleep and grow (fat?) That would be fine if your crowd was to go to the reservoir. And if you thought you really wanted me I could come up Saturday night and go to Wellston from Dayton. I'll have plenty of time and I can't say that I am particularly anxious as to when I go home because I know I'm going to be mighty lonesome after the first few days.

Yes, Esther I am going to town tomorrow and it will be a pleasure indeed to get those pieces for you. I'll have them if they can be had. Have quite a bit of shopping to do to prepare for my vacation.

After all I might be just building air castles again and have them come tumbling down around me at the last minute. Walter, you know, was to work in my place and he will be at Lewis' all next week. He is to see about another job tonight. A friend of my

Dad's is building a new home and Dad spoke to him about carpenter work for Walter. Frank says not to worry about it, that they will get along alright but I just cant help thinking they wont.

I haven't been kidded near so much as I thot I'd be. Maybe they sympathize with me just a little bit – I _am_ mighty lonesome you know. I miss you more than I can say. But I do know I'll get it hot and heavy when I see that Uncle of mine in Elmwood. I don't care – rather like it in fact. Do you think I should make him keep his promise and tell you just how I spend my time as he said he would do? It wont be necessary I can assure you of that, but if you think it would ease your mind any, then of course I'll have him do it. On second thought perhaps I'd better not. It would be just like him to exaggerate and twist things to make them appear to be what they "aint." No Esther, you will have to take my word for it and trust me. By this time I suppose you are thinking that I, too, like to do my share of kidding. Well, maybe I do, and I must admit that some of it is – but only some.

I was up at the barber shop tonight and one of the fellows knowing that I was leaving on my vacation said, "Well, Ralph, you will leave here all _alone_ but I doubt very, very much if you will come back that way." That is just a sample of the kidding I get from that bunch at Lodge since that night I walked up there with you.

Well Esther, write real soon. My regards to all.

Ralph.

Cin'ti O.

9-6-23

Dear Esther:

Certainly was glad to get your letter this morning. Maude and I were both watching for the mailman all morning. Glad to hear you heard from Paul, that's a relief isn't it? And it's fine that his wife is better.

I didn't write last night and we are going to a show tonight so you see I'm trying to write this and work too. Maude is sleeping now so she can stay out late tonight.

43

Everyone is well – But this was a long week till we finally got your letter. Last night we returned the music rolls to the folks in Elmwood and then went down to Lillians and stayed for a couple of hours. From there we went to market. Had quite an enjoyable evening. Coming home we came out past the Fall Festival to see the Tower of Jewels. I wish you could see it Esther. I can't attempt to describe it but it is honestly the most beautiful thing I've ever seen.

We thought of the fudge right after the train pulled out and we both noticed that in the excitement you forgot to kiss Maude good-bye. It wasn't your fault though. And the first thing tuesday morning I looked at the race results to see how much we had won. I wouldn't mind it in the least either to hear the 50¢ bet came across.

I have a nice mess of jiggers too and not only on one leg either. They are getting better now and I hope yours are too. At Frank's suggestion I've been using psychology on them – saying to myself that they don't itch and they aren't there – that may have helped some. Did any of the rest of the crowd get them?

Esther that is mighty sweet of you to get that bill-fold but really you shouldn't have done it. Don't think I don't appreciate it because I do – more than I can say – but it wasn't necessary for you to buy it. You should have given me orders to get one. Now I know I'll always carry my money where it will be safe.

We haven't taken any pictures as yet. I suppose we will have to go up to Walter's place early tomorrow evening to get one of the house. Lou and Julia were to come over last night but didn't. They were to wash today but Mary did it alone. They aren't coming up sunday. I don't know why unless it is because Lou doesn't want to drive that far. Frank may decide later to come but I'll let you know in time what plans are finally made. I may have to send a telegram but I'll get word to you.

Tell your Dad and Mother Ed and Mr & Mrs. Clem hello for me. Regards from all.

Ralph

I'm going to mail this in town tonight so you can get it tomorrow.   Bye.

As ever,

you." Maude knew I was getting letters, but neither one of us ever discussed our letters.

I wasn't working very long at Donenfeld's in the basement of Rike Kumler Com-
pany when they transferred me to the bargain counter (tables end-to-end through the middle of the store). They put me in charge of the bargain tables, and every night I had to see that all of the tables were in shape so that when the doors opened and the people rushed in, the goods were ready to be sold. That usually kept me working an extra hour after everyone else had gone home. I had to go up on the elevator to the differ-ent departments and get the goods that I thought should be out on the tables. I had quit school that year, and when I heard the school bell ring for the first day of school, I was so disturbed. I hadn't known whether I should finish my last year of high school or go to work, but the people at Rike's had promised me a good job on the bargain tables if I would stay, so I took the job. I was so nervous wondering whether I did the right thing, but I didn't have a penny, and Dad never gave us a dime. Looking back on it, I realize taking that job was the best thing that ever happened to me.

"I was dressed up to go to work while Maude tended to chores at home."

Even though Ralph was writing to me, I was so busy working that I didn't think much about boys. I never even knew where a baby came from until I was working at Rike's Department Store on the center counter, and that Edna—whatever her name was—told me that she was going out, and she had to see that she didn't make another baby. I never knew until then that a person got pregnant by laying with a man. She told me, "You go out with a boy, and you'd better be careful or you'll have a baby." Our department-store manager went by and said, "Somebody's telling you stories. Your face is fiery red." I was so em-barrassed. I was never afraid of men or afraid of being with any of them before, but after that, I became real conscious of going with anybody or of anybody getting near me.

Hartwell O.

Sept. 5. [1922]

Dearest Friend:

To say I was glad to hear from you hardly expresses the pleasure with which I received it. But those words do mean a great deal more than one would suppose – sometimes? And I assure you they do to me. Well Esther I was in your City Sunday and Monday, just a very short time on each occasion and I'm kicking myself yet that I didn't stop. At least long enough to say Hello. Went to Columbus Sunday. We had a late start and didn't reach Dayton till 12 noon. Had dinner and even went so far as to go into a phone booth to call you and then decided I had better not do it. Was afraid you had already made plans for the day and I didn't want to be the cause of any disappointment to you. I hope you'll forgive me dear, – I can't forgive my self.

So glad to hear you have learned to drive your machine. Yes, Esther, I did think you was kidding me when you said you wanted to learn to drive. Gee but I would love to teach you – the little that I know. But, dear, your suggestion that I imagine you or Maude beside me is altogether impossible – I can't do it. Have tried and though it is pleasant to allow your imagination to wander at its will and live in your dreams, one can't do it always you know. And however sweet and pleasant those dreams may be they are as nothing compared to the reality. I know because I've experienced both. You have too Esther and don't you agree with me?

I do hope you will become manager of your department. You have all the the qualities making for a good executive, of that I'm sure and I know you will make good in a wonderful way. My heartiest congratulations Esther, dear, and may they be good enough to advance your boss that you too may move up. How I sometimes wish I had started in with an organization where there was a chance for advancement. Here I have gone as far as is possible. The only course left me is to leave altogether in an altogether different line of work or branch out for my self. And I suppose I'll have to do it – self-interest always has been the first law of man and I believe it's only right. I'm sure nobody is going to do for me what they expect me to do for my self.

Do you really and truly hope that we will have those good times together again? At the zoo and playing the piano, I know what you mean, and how well I remember. But how could I forget? I haven't been any place or out with anyone since you left, with the exception of Maudie, of course. Only Saturday Lawrence, my cousin you know, asked me if someone had died. I assured him that everything was allright but he still insists there is something wrong. I agree with him perfectly but it wouldn't do to let him know everything. I now spend my evenings alone in my room with my books – and with my thoughts. I do read an awful lot. I have a set of books, "Masterpieces of Eloquence," ten in all and great large ones at that. You can judge from the title that they are rather dry; but highly interesting they are and I like them.

Do you know Esther I have been at this letter almost an hour and I haven't said anything either have I? I can't put into words what I'd like to say to you. Would sound utterly foolish I think. But may be they wouldn't. Would much rather whisper them in someone's ear. 'Bye dear.

R.

Who did Ralph bring these flowers to, Maude or Esther? Maude remembers they were for her.

Then the government passed a bill enabling employees to be able to get the equivalency of a high school diploma. Businesses were to be reimbursed for company time their employees spent taking courses. So Rike's started a course in salesmanship in the Winters Bank Building for anybody who didn't get to finish the last year of high school. They promised the diploma would be worth as much as any diploma that you could get from high school. They allowed me the time twice a week to go to the Winters Bank Building. Finally, I got my diploma for salesmanship. Then I was promoted to assistant manager of the bargain tables. Later, they moved me to the second floor and wanted me to learn to be the buyer for the Silk and Muslin Underwear Department.

When I was transferred to the second floor at Rike's, I took in fudge. We went into the stockroom, and I gave ev-

Ralph, "Maudie," and Ralph's brother-in-law.

erybody a piece of candy. They all went crazy over it. Everytime I got a chance, I made fudge because I loved the glory of everybody loving the fudge.

I was never certain that Ralph liked me more than Maude until the Christmas of 1923. He got me a cedar chest and asked me to go up to his Aunt Mary Patton's in the country. All of my life I had to have someone with me when I went any place. I was so surprised when Mama let me go to Wellston with Ralph, especially for one whole week. I never said anything to Maude. She probably cried herself to sleep. In all fairness, Ralph talked so little that I don't know how Maude *could* know whether he liked her or me. Only in letters had he said, "I love you, I love you, I can't live without you."

We went to Wellston on the train. I can remember that train ride so plainly. And when we got there, we had to go down an old muddy road to their house. I did have my boots on, but the mud was so deep and sticky that my foot just pulled out of my muddy boot. It was really a rainy, rainy season. We finally got to the house. Aunt Mary's husband had killed a chicken that he had raised, and Aunt Mary prepared it for our meal. Aunt Mary had a summer kitchen—we went down four steps where she made cake donuts. I'll never forget those donuts—nothing ever tasted like that since.

We came home in a taxi, and I think that was the first time Ralph talked about wanting to marry me. When we were alone in the back of the taxi, he was saying how wonderful it would be to be alone with me when we were married.

Soon after we got back home, Mama closed the kitchen door and asked me to stay out. Then Ralph asked her if he could marry me. She answered, "Providing you stay here and don't go away." She thought I was too young to go out on my own. Ralph showed her the ring—just a small diamond. Then Ralph and Mama came out of the kitchen, and Mama put the meal on the table. I don't ever remember him saying, "Will you marry me?" I think he just gave me the ring. I already knew he intended to marry me because of my Christmas present — the cedar chest.

Then Ralph decided if he was getting married, he had to get a good paying job. He took a job with Beech-

"Ralph wanted to get married right away, but Mama said I had to wait until I was twenty-one. I'm wearing my navy-blue with white polka-dot dress. I probably bought it in the basement of Rike's."

nut Packing Company at Youngstown, Ohio. Little did he know—he'd never been away from home—that he could not stand the loneliness of being up there alone. He wrote me and said he couldn't stand it another day, and if they wouldn't let him come back for a week, he would have to quit his job. After seven weeks, he couldn't stand being away any longer. He came down to see me and lost his job. Mother had an extra bedroom and since Ralph had no place to go and no money, she took him in. He was out of work for awhile. Finally, he found a job working for National Biscuit Company. He stayed with us, still treating Maude and me the same. He even kissed Maude—I *saw* him kiss her.

Elmwood Place.

Feb. 18. [1924]

My onliest Sweetieheart.

Just wrote one, dear, to the house but I can't make love to the whole family, can I? Honey I can't be contented any place without you. I miss you so much. I want you — and need you. Each week-end I spend with you makes it just that much harder to be away from you the rest of the week.

I dearly love you honey—suckle; truly and sincerely love you and some sunny day — we are going to see our fondest dreams fulfilled.

I know dear that we will be wonderfully happy because we know and understand each other so well. After our little heart—to heart talk today at lunch I'm sure we could never disagree on anything. At least we could realize our faults and mistakes and forgive and forget.

Darling, I'm going to be awfully lonesome and blue till saturday. I think of you Esther in every waking moment of every day and I have you too, dear, in my dreams. All the love of one who loves you dearly.

Ralph.

3-22-24.

[Youngstown, Ohio]

Just a little love note to my sweetie-heart — the sweetest and dearest girl in all the world. Honey I do love you — love you as never anyone has been loved before. And darling I'll always love you — forever and ever. Esther dear I think of you and dream of you — always — and the day that I can really call you mine, to have and to hold, to love and to kiss, that day darling is going to be the happiest one of my life. And you too honey — don't you often think of how wonderful it's going to be? It would make everything so much easier though dear if we could only be together once in a while. Esther honey I'm so blue and lonesome and homesick, missing you and longing for you. I'm just heart sick dear. I'd sacrifice anything just to be near you — even the prospect of a transfer to Dayton — if it don't come soon enough.

Love & kisses. Ralph.

50

"Esther-O, I love you. Tis yourself knows it's true." – *Ralph*

Youngstown O.

April 19. [1924]

My own darling:

Sweetheart I miss you so and want you so much that if I'm not transferred very, very soon I'm coming to you regardless. I truly love you Esther dearest and I can't live without you. I thoroughly agree with you honeysuckle that life is far too short to live it as we have these past seven weeks – in absolute misery. Seven long, lonesome weeks darling – and it seems that there has been a life time of sorrow and regrets crowded into that seven weeks. Yes darling I do regret that I consented to come up here. But if Stewart keeps his word now and transfers me I will feel that it has been worth it. To be with you always and forever. Darling I'd do anything in the world for you. You are the only one I have ever really loved and I'll always love you Esther.

It will be wonderful to be with you again honey. I'd like, right this very minute, to have one of your smiles – and a kiss. Fifty hundred of them. Good-bye darling for this time but I hope that we will soon be together and happy again.

All my love and kisses for my "baby."

Ralph

Cinti O.   10-30.

My own Sweetheart:

One for just you alone dear – so I can tell you how much I love you. Not that we care who knows how very much in love you and I are. No not that – but I consider it decidedly personal and it would cease to be that if we were to let everyone in on it wouldn't it, honey?

It all seems so wonderful to me darling – and you, dear, you are the most wonderful part of it all. And I do love you – love you with all my heart. It would be humanly impossible for me to love you more. I just couldn't. I fairly idealize you Esther. To me you are the very personification of all that is good and true and beautiful. I've dreamed all my life of the one girl in all the world. And now that I have you sweetheart, that dream has come true. The real girl is even more wonderful than the dream girl.

I am supremely happy when I'm with you honey but it's a long, lonesome week that I have to spend down here without you.

I hope dear you will forgive me for mentioning this, perhaps you will be a bit angry that I did. But I've been thinking of that phone call you had sunday aft. I realize honey that you have given up a great deal, dances and affairs of that sort because you thought I'd expect you to. And frankly I did expect it. I'm just selfish enough to want you all to my self sweetheart. I don't want to share you with anyone. But – please don't think me selfish in any other respect, I'm not I assure you.

This is the first time Esther I've really given it any serious thought. I've come to the conclusion that it isn't right for me to ask you to give up all these things. I think I _know_ you, I trust you, and if you want to go in for dances and parties dear, I haven't the slightest objection. Only a word of unnecessary advice – be careful. Now honey I really mean this – I'm sincere in all of it. It's foolish anyhow to be so insanely jealous – it has wrecked many a happy romance and I'm not so blind as to believe it couldn't do the same to you and I. I love you Esther, always.   Your loving baby,

Ralph.

Maude, Ralph, Esther, Ella, Paul, and Mary Patton.

My own Sweetheart:

Dearest it will be impossible for me to be with you this Sunday but I'm hoping and praying I can soon get back to my "baby". Darling, don't worry about it, please. Soon Honey every-thing will be alright and we will be happy again — all smiles and sunshine. I think of my Esther every minute of the day, and yet I have some wonderful dreams of her too. Oh darling I'd just give anything if I could be with you always — to hold you in my arms again and kiss you and

kiss and kiss you. It has been over a month now dear but it has been a month that seemed a year. I get out your pictures every evening and think and wonder and wish things were different. Honey if such a thing is possible this enforced separation has caused me to love you more. It is a thing so big and so wonderful that I can't begin to write about it. But darling just wait — there are thousands of ways I can show my love when I'm with you. It will seem an eternity until I'm with you again darling. I love only you sweetheart. From your "baby" Ralph.

CINCINNATI, OHIO
FEB 12
1130 PM
1924

REGISTER OR INSURE VALUABLE MAIL

Miss Esther Rohman.
Rike-Kumler Co.
Dayton,
Ohio.

Life went on. When we came home from work, Mama would get the meals. We would eat, do the dishes, and sit on the porch swing, everybody telling of their daily experiences.

We were married the day before Christmas, on December 24, 1924, and Ralph was twenty-four years old. I worked for the Rike Kumler Company, and they wouldn't let me off of work until the twenty-third of December. Standing over the register the morning of my wedding, I was so tired and Mama said, "You can still call it off. You just don't know what you're getting yourself into." I was just from December the 24th to March the sixth of being twenty-one, and Mama wouldn't go to town with us to sign the marriage license. She said we couldn't get married till I was twenty-one. So Dad went with us.

We went down to the courthouse to get our license, and they said Mama had to sign, too. Dad was there. Maude couldn't come; she had to work. Ralph and Dad had to go back home to get Mama. Ralph asked if I wanted to come with them, and I said "No." I knew if I

"Ralph says, 'I love you, Esther.' I am wearing the coat I wore for my wedding. We're standing in the back of Mom and Dad's house on Highland Avenue."

went back home, Mama would not come. Finally, with Mama's signature, we got the permit. Then we went across the street to get married.

They had a chapel especially prepared for weddings in the Winters Bank Building. My brother Paul and his wife, Helen, and Mom and Dad were with Ralph and me. We didn't have but twenty dollars—ten to pay the preacher and ten dollars left. I wore a navy velveteen dress; the edging and the skirt were a light brown. I bought it while I was working at Rike's. I had a real cute tan hat with beads on it and a veil that came down over my shoulders just past my neckline. Ralph wore a suit, and he had his topcoat on. My coat was brown with a pretty fur on the collar and around the edges of the full sleeves.

When we came out of the wedding, Maude saw us from the window of the Credit Union where she worked. Later she said she cried and cried and cried. I didn't realize how much she loved Ralph. Paul threw rice on us. We wanted to go to Cincinnati. We went right over to the train station. The rice was still in my veil and in the fur around my neck, and everybody on the train knew that we had just gotten married. We got to Cincinnati at dusk. It was snowing hard and was bitter cold. We had to stand outside waiting for a taxi, and it seemed as if we had to wait hours. We stayed at the Gibson Hotel—just one night. I had never been with anyone alone. Mama had said only that morning, "You don't know what you're getting into." That scared me. Then when we went downstairs to eat, I was so scared because I had hardly ever eaten out with anyone before. (Ralph was all alone after his mother died and he ate out a lot.) We came back to the room. I was so nervous that the minute Ralph shut the door, I got sick to my stomach and my food came up. On Mama's wedding night she did the same thing. She got so scared that she vomited, too. She had red beets for dinner, and I had red beets.

That night Ralph and I just loved each other as we had before. We really didn't go hardly anyway at all with it. His lodge kept telling the men to respect a woman and not to go ahead and do anything unless it was her wish. I'd always sit on his lap and just love him, and that's what we did then—we just loved each other, only we went to bed. (About two weeks later we found out we hadn't known how.)

We got up early on Christmas Day and went to Ralph's father's home. I was supposed to be Santa Claus for Ralph's youngest brother, Paul Price. They had a red suit for me to wear. It had a cap with white wool on it. I believe they stuck pillows in the front of the suit. As Santa Claus, I just said,

"Ralph was so scared of our dog, but it would do anything for me. He thought it was mean because it didn't like him."

"Ho, ho, ho, ho! Merry Christmas! How are you? Are you a good boy?" Then I passed out nuts and oranges and gave Paul an automobile and other toys.

After we were married, we lived with Mother and Dad. My brother Paul and his wife were in one bedroom; Maude was in the little bedroom in the back. We lived like a family—more like brothers and sisters than husband and wife. After we got married whenever the three of us were together, it seemed as though Ralph treated Maude and me exactly alike. We always sat in that swing on the front porch. I would be on one side of Ralph, Maude on the other. I was more than anxious for Maude to find a husband. One day we had trouble with our stove and called the Power and Light Company. They sent a repair man out. We let him in through the living-room door, and he had to walk through the house to the kitchen. On the piano Mama had pictures of family and friends. He stopped and asked, "How do you happen to have that picture?" Mama answered that it was her mother's brother's daughter-in-law, and he said, "Well, *that's* my sister!" Then they got to talking just like family. His name was Clifton Slye. I told him that Maude wasn't married, and he said he wasn't married either. A few days later, he asked Maude to go on a date with him.

Ralph and I wanted a baby so badly. We took care of my school friend Margaret Barnes McClure's baby that lived next door. We both wanted to dress it and hold it, and my mother said, "You'll have to have more than one baby so that you each can hold one." One rainy Sunday afternoon, Ralph was determined we were going to have a baby, and I think he tried all afternoon. Actually, Ralph was scared that I couldn't have children—Uncle Frank had told him that he'd be really sorry if he married me because I was sickly. Every month I had cramps so bad I couldn't work or do anything; I just was sick and had to go to bed.

Sure enough, on May 25, 1926, we were blessed with two babies, twin girls weighing 6 3/4 pounds and 5 1/2

"Ralph was so proud. He was going to be a father!"

"Ralph and I were blessed with twins. Now we each had a baby to hold. We didn't have a carriage for awhile. Then I found a used double carriage that was bigger than I was. No one could see me when I was pushing it. People would say they didn't know I was behind it."

pounds. For a long time the doctor had told me he was going to have a doctor's party on May 25 and to be sure not to have the baby then. The doctor had estimated the due date of the baby to be February according to my size, not suspecting twins. We had waited from February to May 25. I could hardly walk anymore, I was so much overdue. Mama bought me the largest smock made—a blue cotton with buttons down the front. Every night when we went to bed, we thought that was going to be the one, and I don't know how many times Mama washed everything for the bed thinking the baby was coming that very night. Sure enough, about 2:30 in the morning when the doctor's party was going well, we called him to deliver the baby. After he delivered Evelyn, he said, "You can relax now. It's all over." I said, "Oh, no, it isn't. It's right here yet." "There must be another one then," he said. Ralph was on one side of the bed holding my hand. We had our last penny almost spent. I looked over at him and said, "Honey, do you care? I could make candy and sell it to help out." Then no more was said. I began hemorrhaging. Mama got a great big slop jar and a cup and dipped the blood up. The jar was half full of blood. Supposedly, the healthiest and strongest person could only live seven minutes with that kind of hemorrhage; the doctor needed to deliver the second baby immediately. Dad was walking up and down the hall. When they told him there were twins, he said, "Go back and look. There must be a couple more."

I had blood poisoning within a couple of days. The doctor said it was time for his vacation so I switched to Dr. Prugh. He sent away by plane for a miracle drug and said that was the only thing that saved my life.

The first week after the twins were born, Ralph was excited about going out to get something to eat with his cousin and his wife. He lit up a cigarette and put the match underneath the faucet so fast that the water didn't put it out. Then he threw the match into the waste basket under the stairway. After Ralph went out, it all went up in flames. The fire went straight up the stairs. I was in bed with the twins with blood poisoning. When Ralph came back to Mama and Dad's house, the fire department was there with the ladder up to the window of our bedroom. The firemen were wondering whether they would take me and the babies out the window, but then they got the fire out. Ralph was so embarrassed. After all, Dad had told me not to marry that "cigarette-smoking skinny flint"— Dad was so against anybody who smoked a cigarette. Of course, smoking a cigar or chewing tobacco, as he did, was alright.

"Ralph was so anxious to show everybody the twins. I told him that the sunlight would be too bright for the babies' eyes. But Ralph didn't listen, he was just so proud."

59

"I took care of the twins and did the housework during the day and made candy while they were sleeping at night."

Chapter Three

Take my fudge and wrap it up in chocolate.

When I got married, the girls at Rike's said they would miss the fudge I brought in to eat, and if I would make it, they would buy it. I didn't do anything about it the months I was pregnant. I didn't think anymore about making candy, or selling candy, until we were blessed with twins. We were living with Mom and Dad and Maude. Everybody was holding a baby. Maude was always holding Evelyn. She said I should share—I had two, and I ought to give Evelyn to her. She wanted Evelyn and wasn't going to take "no" for an answer.

Ralph was working, but it seems that even then the money didn't go around. We didn't have a dime. He got paid twice a month. When I would get the check cashed, I would put seventeen cents under one cup because, by the end of the month, we were out of his cigarette money. I knew Ralph couldn't live without his cigarettes so I always hid that money. At that point I wasn't selling candy yet so I never got any money back. Then the girls that I had worked with at Rike's called and asked me if I had made any more candy, that they had a bunch of employees that would buy it if I would make it. I thought I could make fudge to help pay the bills and called the one girl at Rike's. She got an order together for twenty-three

"Ralph is holding Eileen, I am holding Evelyn. We are sitting on the running board of our Whippet automobile."

62

"Evelyn and Eileen enjoyed each other's company as identical twins. They could communicate with each other without even speaking."

pounds real quick. Everybody wanted it.

I had two shopping bags, one on each side of me, and I was very conspicuous. The head floorman that I had known for years caught me with the two bags of candy and asked, "What have you got in there?" And I said, "Candy for the girls. They called me and said they wanted some." And he said, "Now you know you can't bring candy in here to sell. If our employees want it, we'll sell it from the candy counter." He took me over to the candy counter. They opened a package and tasted it and said yes, they would sell it. All the girls that were waiting for me to come in with their pound of candy had to go down to the candy shop to get it. Rike's doubled the price, and everybody had to pay that to get the pound of fudge that I had made for them. From that day on, Rike's said they would buy candy from me.

Everyday when the store closed, Rike's would call and tell me how much fudge they needed for the next day. I didn't realize I was not strong enough to take on that much responsibility while I was still recovering from a severe case of blood poisoning after the birth of the twins. The twins didn't always sleep very well. Sometimes it was late before I had them fed and in bed; then I would first put on the fudge. I didn't get to make as much candy as I needed, and I was under such a strain worrying whether the twins were going to wake up and whether I would finish making the candy before they woke up. Mama stayed up many nights with me making that fudge. It was just plain chocolate fudge. I didn't use nuts because it would make the price too high. I used the cream from the milk company—the thin cream. Ralph, in no way, would get involved with the candy—he didn't want to even know that I was making candy then.

Finally Rike's ordered fudge one night, and I couldn't get it made for the next day. I was sick—just exhaustion all the way through me from never getting any sleep and from working and worrying about the candy. The doctor said I had a heart attack, and that I would never be able to work a whole day again. Then Rike's ordered fudge from another person because after they started selling fudge, everybody wanted fudge.

I had been wanting to buy a house of our own because I was keeping everyone awake when I was making candy at night. And I wanted to be by ourselves—finally alone with Ralph. There were just too many people at the house. Ralph kept saying, "We absolutely cannot buy a house at all." We had already bought a lot out by Wright-Patterson Air Force Base. They signed us up and then we paid so much a month. By the time I wanted to buy a house, we had the lot almost paid for. Then without Ralph's knowledge, I found a builder who said he would take the lot as a down payment on the house that I liked on Fauver Avenue. The bank found a second mortgage investor for the balance that was still owed. We would only have to make a monthly payment. It was the first house finished in a rural neighborhood, and there appeared to be lots of room. Mama was so upset. There were ponds all around; Dad always went there hunting. "Oh, you won't be going to that God-forsaken duck-hunting grounds," she said. But we bought the house on Fauver Avenue anyway. We moved in, buying only the necessary pieces of furniture to get by on: the stove, refrigerator, and a good, old iron skillet.

When I started making fudge again, I told the people who called me and wanted it to come out to the house to get it. People heard about it. They'd come out, and I'd take them into the house and pack their candy. I was not allowed to have a sign out front so I had the house number put on the front post with illuminated red numerals so that they would show up better. Ralph yelled right away, "Are you bringing the Red-light District up here?" That struck me like a bolt of lightning—I had never thought of that. There was a Red-light District on Xenia Avenue, not too far from the house. I called the electrician who had put the number in and told him to change the light to blue. From then on when anybody called for directions, I told them to watch for the blue-lighted numbers.

"Evelyn, Eileen, Jack, and I on the front steps of Fauver Avenue. Jack tried to scoot out of my arms. He didn't want to sit still a minute—he always wanted down."

All this time I was only making fudge. I'd make the candy at night, cut it up, put it into pound packages, and wrap it in wax paper. Then I'd put the candy into two shopping bags and walk twelve blocks to the streetcar stop. The minute I'd put the twins to bed, the next-door neighbor would open her windows so she could hear the babies when they cried. Then she would take care of them until I got home. I went from door to door downtown, but mostly to banks and doctors' offices. I went to the bank first. I knew about what time the twins would wake up, so I hurried to get rid of the candy I had. When I'd sell what I could sell and I knew it was time to go home, I would go to Dr. Prugh's office. He'd take the side of the shopping bag and say, "How many have you got left?" And I'd say, "I don't know." He'd just toss me some money

"The twins grew so fast that before I had time to shorten the hem on Evelyn's coat, I needed to let the hem back out on Eileen's coat. The candy business was keeping me busier all the time."

and say, "Now go home and feed the babies." And I'd hurry home to take care of them. Many times I would get home before they woke up. If not, the neighbor would hear them crying and come over and talk to them, playing with them on the floor for awhile.

I remember one time when the twins were only a couple of months old. It took me longer than usual to sell the candy, and it was past time for me to nurse the twins. It was pouring down rain, and I was waiting for a streetcar to go home. A machine pulled up at the curb. A man motioned with his hand for me to come to the car. It was raining so hard that I couldn't see who it was. All I saw was his hand, and I thought someone I knew had come to meet me because I was late to nurse the babies. I got into the car and first realized I didn't know the person. He was young and clean cut, but he said he was going to take me to Cincinnati, and I said, "Oh, no! I can't go. I have twins and it's time for me to nurse them." He continued to drive, and I pleaded, "Oh, please let me out. Oh, please let me out." But he said, "I can *make* you go. I have a gun underneath the front seat." I was so scared that I yelled, "Please let me out at this corner! I can catch my streetcar here." I felt like screaming with happiness when he stopped and let me out.

On one of my trips downtown, Dr. Prugh said, "Take my piece and wrap it up in chocolate," and I said, "Oh, I don't know how. It might turn gray." "I don't care if it would turn green," he said. "If you made it, it would still be good." So I ran to the grocery store and got what they had on the shelf to dip the chocolate in—Walter Baker's Chocolate, the one-pound, twenty-five-cent bars. I hurried home and melted it. Well, that naturally was a little too bitter, so I got some milk chocolate to mix with it. I mixed the Walter Baker's Semi-sweet with the milk chocolate. That gave it a very good flavor. All the time I would mix the chocolate and try to dip it and, oh boy, it was good and it did turn gray, but I didn't know much about it then. It turned color and it wasn't a pretty shine, but we ate it anyway.

Then I made more until I learned that I was melting the chocolate at too high of a temperature. After I melted my chocolate, I wasn't letting it cool down enough before I dipped it. I found out afterwards that chocolate shouldn't be heated much higher than melting temperature, and when you dip it, it has to be cooled down until it's almost ready to set up into a solid piece of chocolate. If you didn't go fast enough (or have warmer chocolate to mix with it), the chocolate you were working with would set before you got it dipped. All the time you had to add a little more melted chocolate to it, but by buying only that one pound of chocolate, I didn't have enough chocolate to really work it right. Finally, I learned that you pour a little chocolate out on a marble slab like icing on a cake and work it with your hand. As soon as that sets, you scrape it up and mix it with a little more melted chocolate. That makes the seed that helps it to set with a gloss.

I learned that humidity bothered chocolate, too. I couldn't have all the doors open. I didn't have air-conditioning so I had to do my dipping in the mornings, in the evenings—after the sun went off the roof.

At the end of my second pregnancy I was so big that, to beat the fudge, I had to have the kettle out on the end of my knees. The doctor insisted that I had to go to the hospital this time. He said, "The same thing follows through," meaning that I might hemorrhage again as I did with the twins. I wanted the baby to come on a Saturday night while Ralph was home from work because the twins were scared of nearly everybody else. The doctor said, "Now take it easy and *don't* get down and scrub the floor—that might cause your water to break." So I scrubbed the floor on Saturday on purpose and took a bath. I no more than lay down and my water broke. I couldn't even get my socks and shoes on. Ralph took me to the hospital. He dropped me off at the door and then hurried back home because the twins were there alone, asleep. A nurse took me in. The doctor was running down the hall after me. He knew that after having twins, the second baby would come soon. Jack was born about an hour and a half after I got to the hospital, early Sunday morning, on March 3, 1929. The doctor had promised if everything was okay, he'd allow us to come home that same day. We went home later that day in the afternoon.

We had the house for a couple of years. Then during the Depression, we weren't able to make our payments and were going to lose it. A law came in that the government would loan money if you didn't have a second mortgage or if you had everything else clear on it. Unfortunately, we had a second mortgage on it, and the woman had moved to California. I tried to borrow the money, but I couldn't get it unless I had that second mortgage released. I got in touch with the mortgage holder. She didn't do anything about it for a long time. Then at the last minute I wrote to her again. Her lawyer told her either I would lose the whole thing and she would never see any money, or she could release the second mortgage, and if I got anything, I'd pay her. She sent me the second mortgage clear at the last second. We had our boxes packed and near the door. Jack was sitting on them anxiously waiting to see the moving truck. Ralph had rented a place where fifteen people used one bathroom right by the Biscuit Company. He had heard about it and taken it right away. We were supposed to move into that place. But the woman in California saved our life. Then, after we got the home loan from the bank, we had money enough to pay her back.

I could continue my candymaking. I poured it in pans on the kitchen table and carried it onto the dining-room table when it was time for us to eat in the kitchen. Then when I wanted to cut it up, I'd carry it back to the kitchen table again. I was constantly carrying candy back and forth from the kitchen to the dining room. A lot of times, I'd have the dining-room table full of candy with just one cloth over all of it. I was always doing my dishes late in the evening. Out of the corner of my eye I would see a shadow going across the dining room and back. I thought Jack was asleep, but he would get out of bed, sneak into the dining room, and get handfuls of candy. When I'd make his bed in the morning, I'd find a handful of candy under his pillow that he hadn't eaten yet.

Dad always stopped on his way home from Frigidaire to see how I was getting along. He was so thrilled that I was making candy, and he would tell

Jack with his puppy and twin sisters.

everybody he knew about it. He'd stop in to see what I had made, and he'd take it in to the men at the company.

I was only experimenting with dipping then. When I really started dipping, I bought ten-pound cakes of chocolate. Normally, a company wouldn't sell as little as fifty pounds. You had to buy larger quantities. Hershey's did sell me fifty pounds in one big carton. Then I went to Walter Baker's and then to Nestles, and I liked Nestles the best.

My pieces of candy were about the size of a golf ball—there were about seven pieces to a pound. Then some lady said, "I've got a bunch of company coming and this box of candy doesn't go around. Take mine and make little pieces for me." So I took that pound of candy and made as small of pieces as I could (just regular size) and dipped them for her. She liked them so much and told others, and from then on I made both sizes of candy to sell.

When I had to make more candy, my wrist wouldn't hold out for the beating of it. My wrist would crack every time I attempted to beat it. I tied my wrist tightly, but it still cracked, and it wouldn't beat the fudge. Finally, my wrist gave out, and I couldn't beat the candy anymore by hand. I was searching constantly for a beater that was strong enough to beat fudge. But fudge is about as tough as it gets. Fudge even gets tougher than bread dough. I found the Mixmaster and I was thrilled. I thought that would do it, but it just growled when it went to beat the fudge. It wasn't strong enough so I got the largest Mixmaster, and that wouldn't do it. Then I went to a wholesale house and got a bread mixer—a big bowl that had a dough hook. I bought that on time; I could pay by the month. When they delivered the mixer, I told them to set it right there in the kitchen where I was making the candy (I made the candy on the kitchen stove and set it out on the back porch or carried it down into the basement onto the cement floor to cool). The delivery man said, "Oh, no, this little floor will never hold that. With the vibrations it will wear right through the floor and end up in the basement. You've got to take that onto the basement concrete floor." They nearly broke their backs getting that heavy mixer down the narrow stairway. I never will forget—they had no equipment to do it with, and there were just the two men.

I got six hot plates and lined them up so that I could put six kettles on at once. I had a spoon in each kettle. I stirred with both hands, and I could stir this kettle and the next kettle and go up and down the rows. When the kettles were finished, I didn't even test them. By that time I could tell by the bubble whether it was finished or not. If it had a thick, popping bubble, it was finished. Then I'd set that kettle onto the floor until I had all six kettles off to cool. I had six pans that were the same size, and I put the same

"Myrtie Freese [right] was my first dipper. She worked for me for nearly forty years. Little did I know that she would become Evelyn's mother-in-law."

amount into each pan. Then I let the candy cool until it was just at the beating stage.

Then someone reported to the Board of Health that I was making candy in the basement. I had just spent all that money on the beater, and they came out and said, "No, no, no! You have to enclose this, and you have to enclose that, and you have to put water here." I nearly died when I knew all the money I had to spend just to make that candy. Fortunately, Ralph's father's brother, Uncle Watt, heard that I needed help and came up from Cincinnati to build the partitions. He had lost his arm in the coal mines and didn't have a steady job, but he was so great at doing any kind of construction work.

I put a table in one room so that I could dip. I dipped late into the night whatever I got cooked. Soon I found out that a lady at church, Myrtie Freese, was a dipper. She came to work for me right away. She was the only dipper I had for quite awhile. [Evelyn would grow up and fall in love with Myrtie's son, Herb, who came to the candy store to pick up his mother after work.] After I moved to the basement, I could not hear the customers at the door. I'd be in the middle of stirring candy, and I couldn't leave. Most generally there was someone waiting on the next piece I made. They just had to come in, and if I had it, alright. I never knew how much I was going to get made. I knew the people so well. They were like family and friends, and I felt terrible when I didn't have the candy for them. But at Christmastime I never could make enough.

By four o'clock in the afternoon the day before Christmas, I would think most of the customers had already been there, and I would rush out and buy the children all the presents I could before the stores closed. When I got back, I always was surprised that there still were more people wanting candy. People kept coming late into the evening. Ralph and I still had the Christmas tree to put up before we could go to bed. (I always told the children that Santa Claus and his elves put the tree up, and if Santa Claus thought you saw him, he would leave.) One time it was 2:30 in the morning when we were decorating the tree. The neighbors were coming home from a party, and they stopped in and talked so loudly that they woke the children. They saw us decorating the tree instead of Santa Claus. I always had a big spruce tree. It didn't seem like Christmas without the smell of pine. Ralph put it in a base, straightened it, and then put the lights on it. Then

"I left for town with the three children and a shopping bag of candy on each arm. I left the twins standing in front of the Fidelity Bank and took Jack inside with me while I sold candy to the employees. When I sold all of the candy, I would buy Jack a little car and the girls a paper-doll book. Then we'd go home on the streetcar."

we put the ornaments on. I was so tired that I just threw the aluminum icicles all over the tree to finish it. Then I set the presents underneath without wrapping them—little cars and other toys for Jack, dolls and identical clothes for the girls. When everyone was taking their tree down, I was first having time to enjoy mine. I always said that candymakers should have their Christmas a week later. I never took the tree down until almost all of the needles had fallen off. About the end of January, Ralph would become so embarrassed that somebody would see our tree was still up.

I first tried to borrow money from People's bank, but they wouldn't loan me a dime. They wouldn't loan women without a large bank account any money. They said, "When you get money in the bank, then we'll loan you some." And I said, "Then I won't need it." In general, the banks would not loan a woman any money at this time. I never was able to borrow except from people that I knew. The first money I tried to borrow was for the big mixer. I had to get the money from friends or anybody that would help me. I was constantly searching for somebody to loan me enough money to make candy. I asked everybody. I talked and talked. That was the only way I could get by. I didn't make that much money from the candy, and what I did make went back into expanding the house and buying machinery, so I was always in debt. I paid whatever interest the people would ask, but most generally it was not much over the amount asked by the bank. In the candy business you have to make candy so far ahead for the different seasons. I only made what I could make, and then I had to quit until I sold the first of the candy. When I got that money back, I could make some more candy.

On Fauver Avenue the people came in through the front door and I sold the candy from the living room. The candy was packed on the enclosed back porch. We never quit making candy until the children were out of school for the summer, and I didn't start again until the children went back to school—it was impossible to make candy with everybody running through the house. After the twins were married, we made our bedroom into the candy room, and we took the upstairs room for our bedroom. We used the front bedroom for packing. In the summertime I'd take the candy out of the front room and make that room into our bedroom. Then when September came, I'd carry the furniture upstairs. It seems I was always carrying furniture upstairs and downstairs.

From the time Jack was young, he helped me in the candy business. As soon as he could pull a wagon up the street, Jack went around the neighborhood with a wagon full of candy and a pocketbook full of coins. The neighbors bought the candy of their choice and made their own change. I had a pile of boards that somebody had given to me. When

Jack was very young, I gave him some nails and a hammer, and he made a rack for me that I used for years. He seemed to be so gifted—he could repair anything. When he was twelve-and-a-half, I bought him a car to work on to keep him busy and close to home. He took it apart and put it back together many times; finally he got it fixed so he could drive me to the country to get cream. Then I got him a special license when he was only fourteen so that he could drive me where I needed to go.

From the time I started making candy, Ralph wanted me to stop. He thought I shouldn't make candy because his boss said that National Biscuit Company paid them enough money so that the wives didn't have to go out of the home to work, that it would look bad for National Biscuit. He said that if any woman was working, the company would fire the man. The one fellow's wife worked for the telephone company, and they did fire him. Ralph was scared to death that if I made candy, he'd get fired, too. The Biscuit Company said the wife could not work, Ralph insisted. In those years Ralph never had anything to do with taking anybody candy because of the threat of losing his job. I never knew when Ralph was coming home from work. Many times when I'd see him coming down the driveway, I'd hurry up and shove that kettle of candy into the cupboard thinking he wouldn't smell it. He went on past and didn't pay any attention—smells didn't mean anything to him. Finally, National Biscuit Company hired a new manager that Ralph really liked.

"Ralph worked extra hours to be the best salesman for National Biscuit Company. He was afraid he might lose his job if I sold candy. He said, 'Esther, you can't make candy.' "

Ralph was no longer afraid that he would get fired because I made candy. The manager visited us and liked the candy so much that he wanted to buy some for his family.

When I decided to dip the candy, I left the chocolate out of some of it and made some plain white buttercream—opera cream. I made it just the same, except for the chocolate. I took part of the buttercream and made Easter eggs. I didn't know where to go with all of those eggs. They weren't something that I could make and wrap and put away to sell. I had to let them set, then decorate them, wrap them, put Easter grass in boxes, and then the eggs down into them. After cooking all that candy, the basement got too hot and steamy to let the eggs set out. I could only dip the eggs when it was cool enough because the chocolate had to be a certain degree. I had an unfinished room in the attic, but there were loose boards on the floor. I decided that I could use that space, but the problem was I needed tables. I asked Ralph to bring home some large Shredded Wheat cartons. I turned them on their sides and then took some boards from the floor and used them across the cartons for tables for my Easter eggs. I only wanted one table, and he brought the cartons for that, and I took the boards off the floor and made a table. Immediately, I saw that I needed more tables. I asked for more Shredded Wheat cartons and made the attic full of tables to put my candy on. I would make the candy in the basement and carry it to the attic to be dipped and decorated. It was cool enough outside that the candy was okay up there. It seemed as if the first day of September, when the children went back to school, it turned cool and never got hot after that—it never fluctuated like it does today.

In order to melt my chocolate for the Easter eggs, I used large pans for a double boiler and just got the chocolate warm—you could not melt it fast; you just had to keep stirring it. Once you got a little bit melted, you could bury a piece of chocolate and the rest of that would melt fast. Then I had to cool that down to dipping temperature—just to lukewarm. I had a marble slab that I had received from a neighbor, and I would put my chocolate out on that. Thousands of pounds of candy were dipped on that.

I made the fudge with cocoa and sugar and cream—a light cream. At first, when I used small amounts, I got cream from the grocery store. Then the milkman came every morning from the dairy. He brought from two quarts to whatever I ordered depending on how much candy I could make. We had a milkbox on the porch, and I'd put a note in it listing what I wanted. Later on, I contacted a dairy and had a dairy deliver it. When I started making candy on a large scale, every Friday my son, Jack, would drive me to different farms and get heavy cream. Later, I bought a Guernsey cow for Maude and her husband. [Yes, after many years of courtship, Cliff and Maude were married. They had a big church wedding and Maude wore a white wedding gown and veil. The twins were old enough to attend and remember the wedding.] They brought me the milk to pay for the cow. When one cow was paid for, I bought them another cow. Finally, they ended up with eight cows. Cliff and Maude got up at four o'clock every morning, milked the cows, and brought the milk into the candy store.

First, I bought the gallons of milk, let them set, took off the cream, and made my butter out of all the excess cream that I had. Later on, I bought plain gallons of cream, especially when I needed to make butter. I would only go to farms that had Guernsey cows because they gave the best cream. It was much thicker. At first we had an ice box.

"I carried all of these Easter eggs from the basement to the attic and put them on my makeshift tables. Then I dipped and decorated them. I made choco-late, buttercream, coconut, pecan, fruit-and-nut, and peanut-butter ones."

I had to use the cream right away. Whatever turned a little bit sour, I made butter out of—that's when I started making my butter—whenever I had an excess of cream. I had to have the butter in crocks—I couldn't have it in aluminum. I had a little wooden churn. With Guernsey cream, it seemed like it made butter after just a few turns.

I wanted a variety of pieces for my boxes of candy. I added nuts to the buttercream. In some of the candy I added ground coconut. I put peanut butter inside a piece of white buttercream. I took the soft cream, which was very hard to handle, spread it out like pie dough, covered it with as much peanut butter as it would hold, and then rolled it to the right thickness. Then the dippers would pinch off a piece with their left hand while they were dipping with their right hand. I took a piece of cream and put a cherry into it, pinched it shut like you do an apple dumpling, and then gave it a roll as I tossed it down. Everybody liked chocolate covered cherries because the longer the cherries stood, the more juice they got in them. The cherries and peanut butters were the extra-size pieces in the boxes.

We loved peanut brittle. I made it from the very beginning. I would put sugar, water, and corn syrup together. I didn't put butter in peanut brittle because it wouldn't

The girls were young when Esther would send them outside to find her a four-leaf clover. She put it in the heel of her shoe and then went to the horse races. Ralph did not know about it, Esther thought. "On one of those days, he came out there and found me. On that same day a whole lot of horses fell down and were killed and they were the ones that I had bet on, and I said, 'You made my horses fall down.' Ralph thought I was meeting a man, but I was only meeting Margaret Barnes."

be as crispy—you needed it to be so crisp and thin that when you'd touch it, it would break. I got raw peanuts and cooked them in the syrup as it was boiling. I kept out a cup and a half of peanuts and ground them. Just before the peanut brittle was finished, I gave it about four-to-five minutes of cooking the ground peanuts in the candy. When it was getting brown around the side and I knew it would burn if it cooked another minute, I added baking soda and vanilla, then beat it like the dickens, and poured it out on the slab. Then I'd take the spatula and lay half of it over here and half of it over there so that it wasn't too thick. Within seconds I went all around the outside edge where it was too thick. I'd pull it real thin, just pulling it out about an inch, and I had somebody working on the other side because it would set up quickly. When I pulled that one piece off, I had another tray buttered so that I could lay that piece onto it. I had trays buttered all around so that when I pulled the pieces as thin as paper, I could lay those onto another

"During the 1952 open house for the new Wayne Avenue store, the crowds came to sample all of my different candy and to see it hand-dipped. I was cutting caramel, which was everybody's favorite. There were ten pounds of butter and heavy whipping cream in every batch."

tray until I got to the very center of it. The peanut brittle cooled so fast that I could hardly keep up with stretching it thin. Then it was ready to be put into sacks. If I didn't get it into sacks immediately, the humidity would get it damp right away. Then I found that if I had a stainless-steel table to pour it on, I could start on all the outside edges and pull it thinner. The second the pieces were pulled out thin, I could break them off and lay those onto another table, then pull the next off until I had loads of peanut brittle from that one pan. And everybody loved it stretched thin. One time I put my peanut brittle on the back porch to cool. When I went to get it, some boys had taken all the candy from the back porch. I had that order sold. I needed it—people were coming after it. I had to make another batch. I don't remember making any more peanut brittle after that because it made so much confusion, and I was so short of space. When I did get it made, I would put it into sacks, and the children would take it to the neighbors and sell it right away. That's why it was so good—it was sold just minutes after I got it off the stove.

I just loved the caramels. I started making them on the kitchen stove. Caramels had to be stirred every minute for an hour over the gas stove. I doubt if the girls were seven years old when they would help me. "Oh, not again," they'd say. Everybody else got to play, but they had to stir the candy. They had two chairs at the stove and their wooden spoons, and they'd stir that candy until it got thick and started popping. Then I finished the caramels. I put gloves on because it would pop on my hands. Sometimes it would pop all over the kitchen. Then the next day when the caramel was cooled, Evelyn and Eileen had to wrap the caramels in the basement.

Most everything went by sight with me. I could tell how thick the bubble was on it—it left the edge of the pan a little bit when it started to get done. With the caramel I would put the butter in right away—I wouldn't wait until it was getting nearly done. I used heavy cream and condensed milk—one-third condensed milk, half-brown and half-white sugar, according to how much I was cooking, and a whole cup of corn syrup—and it had to be the heavy kind; otherwise, I had to cook the water out of it too long. I was getting fifty-pound kegs of corn syrup. I put vanilla in when the caramel was almost finished but still cooking. I cooked it until it was so ready to burn that I could see the brown—the caramel getting a little darker. Then I poured the caramel out into big trays and let it cool and couldn't disturb it or cut it until the next day. It was not until my candy kitchen on Wayne Avenue that I got the large automatic copper kettle. That was such a miracle after years of stirring an hour over each batch of that caramel. I just put all of the ingredients into the copper kettle, put the arm down, set the timer, and went away. I doubled my recipes as I made bigger batches.

I had bought an ice-cream freezer when I worked at Rike's. Since I didn't make candy in the summer, sometimes I would make pineapple sherbet. I always cooked my sherbet like custard with milk and eggs, sugar, cornstarch, vanilla, and a pinch of salt. First, I soaked a couple of tablespoons of gelatin in a large crock. Then I stirred part of the sugar with the cornstarch and a pinch of salt and thinned it with a little milk. If you put too much sugar in your custard, it will separate and it won't thicken, so I added it separately. Next, I would whip up the eggs and add them to the cornstarch mixture. I would have milk heating on the stove, and just before it came to a boil, I would slowly add the thickening, stirring it constantly. Still stirring, I would turn the fire very low and let it cook, not over ten minutes. Then I added the cooked custard to the crock of gelatin. I didn't cook it anymore. I added the juice of four lemons and a large can of crushed pineapple for a two-gallon ice-cream container. I added the rest of the sugar (some of it I had cooked in the custard part) to my mixture. I added a little more milk—it was good Guernsey milk so it was almost like cream. If I didn't have Guernsey milk, I used cream.

On our first attempt at a vacation, I decided we should go to Cedarville Lake, the place that Ralph's boss had suggested. We had just had a little batch of puppies, and we had to take the puppies with us. With all of it together, Ralph was just about to go crazy. It took awhile for me to get everything ready for the children and then to get the box of puppies ready. And I had to pack all of the pots and pans and everything for living up there. We lost a box of something on the way and had to go back and hunt for it because

"I stopped candymaking for the summer and we were off for our first family vacation to Cedarville Lake. We tied boxes onto the running board of the car, which was already filled with three children, three puppies, and their mother, Fluffy. When we were almost there, the rope broke and a box fell off the running board into a ditch. Ralph went to hunt for it and was so frustrated."

79

"Jack and Ralph at Maude and Cliff's farm, where they had the Guernsey cows."

Below: Esther and Ralph with the twins (Evelyn on left, Eileen on right) and Jack.

they had tied it onto the running board. Then, when we finally got up there, I told Ralph to go out and fish. I thought he'd be happier if he didn't see me unload all that—until I got the beds made and something on to eat. Oh, when I think about all the work.... He took all three of the children out in the boat. He was casting into the lily pads with a huge, three-pronged hook. He didn't notice that the wind had turned the boat. He was still casting in the same direction. I heard all three children scream at once; everybody around the lake heard them scream. The hooks went into Eileen's head. Ralph shook so bad. Right away he came in from the lake, and we took Eileen to find a doctor. We had to go to three different doctors until we could find a surgeon to cut the hooks out.

The second attempt for a vacation was the next year. On the Fourth of July holiday, we went to Lake Erie. Ralph hadn't wanted to go. We stayed with Maude and Cliff. Since the sun wasn't shining, we thought we couldn't get sunburned but Ralph got a severe case of sunburn. By five o'clock that first day, he was in severe chills and very sick. I decided we had to turn around and go home that very night, and I started driving with traffic bumper-to-bumper on two-lane roads. It was at least a six-hour trip. (I had only driven a car once before. Ralph had a little Ford coupe that he had used to go to work. Someone dared me to drive it, and I thought I knew how. I got in it and started driving, and then I didn't know how to stop. I got so weak from fear that I let my foot off the pedal, and it stopped just before hitting a car. But I had sat beside Ralph and watched him drive, and I just took for granted that I knew how.) I got stopped right on the railroad track and there was a train coming. Ralph was so sick, but he told me to pull up and push the car ahead of me. The man came back and was going to fight Ralph. It seems as though he had something from his car that he was going to beat us with. Some truck driver got out and helped us. After a couple of days Ralph couldn't even stand up on his feet; his legs just buckled under him. I called the doctor. He said it would take at least two weeks to draw the sun out of his bones. The doctor told me to put hot Epson salts towels on it! For two weeks Ralph couldn't even get out of bed.

I had a 1940 Chrysler sedan I got from Dad. Someone gave me a baby calf. I made up my mind to take it to Ralph's brother and wife, Duke and Edna. Their house had just burned down, and they were building a house with no money. They wanted a cow that they could milk. I got the calf into the Chrysler. The head was out one door of the car, the tail out the other door. Then it began fertilizing the upholstery. It made Jack sick seeing that new car like that. He worked and worked to get the upholstery clean, but he *never* could get the smell out.

Fauver Avenue was only a two-bedroom house. There were five in the family; in addition Ralph's Aunt Mary Patton had come to live with them. She cooked for the family. The twins were now teenagers. The candy business had really grown. Esther fixed up the basement and had at least four dippers dipping in one corner down there. It was there in the basement that the twins listened to the adult gossip and off-color jokes.

Evelyn and Eileen helped dip nuts. One night at Christmas time, Esther sent the twelve-year-olds down to dip some nuts for a customer who wanted a box of chocolate-covered pecans. The dippers had been saying that chocolate was so good for your skin. So the girls covered their arms and faces with chocolate. "I had a customer waiting on

a pound of nuts, and I went downstairs. As expensive as that chocolate was, they had put it on their face and arms! I was furious!"

Ralph had bought a new car. Finally, after a couple of years he had it paid off, and he was so happy. It was the greatest thing in the world to him. He came home for lunch and told Esther his good news. That very next day she went downtown and borrowed all the money she could on it. When he found out, he was furious.

During World War II, I could not make any candy unless people traded their sugar with me. They would bring me two pounds of sugar and want me to make candy. But I didn't know whether it was cane sugar or beet sugar. Beet sugar was shinier and harder—I could almost tell by looking at it, and whenever I mixed the cane sugar with the beet sugar, it would make my whole batch go to sugar. People would bring me two pounds of sugar and think they should get much more candy out of it. Then keeping track of how much sugar each person brought me was really a problem. Sometimes two families would go together and bring me the sugar the whole family got because they said they only used it in their coffee or tea.

When people came to buy candy, they talked to me. They wanted to know how I made candy and visit longer than I had time. They'd tell me about the piece of candy they liked the best. I didn't have any certain hours that I was open. Most people came before or after work. People came so late that I almost wished they would stop. They were just passing by and thought they'd take a chance on stopping in, or they had just got out of a meeting and thought I might still be up. My main idea was to let them pick up their own candy and make their own change. Uncle Watt came and built a front porch for me. We built it up halfway with brick like the house and then put in big picture windows all the way across the front. I put a piece of board the length of the porch for the table. Then I had every kind of candy I had finished. I would put twenty dollars worth of change in an old wooden cigar box. I discovered I could make a whole batch of candy in the time it took to sell one box. Then to my surprise, I had to buy awnings because the sun shining on the glass melted my candy.

We always had a big dish of samples on the table. When anybody came in, we'd give them a sample. Once, a man asked if he could take the dish out to his mother. He brought it back—empty.

For our twenty-fifth wedding anniversary, Ralph traded my small diamond ring in on a bigger one.

In the summer of 1950, Ralph had his first heart attack. He was taken to the hospital. When Ralph was in the hospital, Esther would not let him take as many pills as they were giving him. She flushed the pills down the toilet until the nurses finally realized what was going on. They were measuring his intake and output, but Esther was feeding him. She was having her daughter Eileen come up the back steps of the hospital with carrot and celery juice and homemade apple sauce. The nurses began wheeling Ralph out to

Above: Herb Freese on a date with Evelyn in front of Fauver Avenue house.

Right: Evelyn was married to Herb on June 15, 1946.

Below: Six weeks after Evelyn's wedding, Eileen married William Otto. Esther baked and decorated the wedding cake.

Ralph recovering at Bear Lake.

the nurses' center to give him his pills. That's when Esther decided to take him out of the hospital. It was time to quit candymaking for the year, and she thought if she could just get him up to Bear Lake, Michigan, he could rest and he'd recover. Esther got him dressed and wheeled him out; she didn't ask for a release. The doctor said he was off the case. Jack was waiting with the car. They took him to the lake, fixed a hammock for him to lie in, and Esther nursed him back to health. Esther spent entire mornings cleaning celery, carrots, and parsley, and making juice. After six weeks Ralph looked so good that everybody thought he hadn't had a heart attack after all. The very next day after they got home, he went back to work. But six weeks later Ralph had another heart attack— this time much worse than the first one. Esther was making candy and nursing him, too. After working there twenty-seven years, National Biscuit Company put him on disability. For years, Ralph did the candy-store bookwork, keeping the business organized while continuously worrying about the tremendous bills for new additions and machinery. Ralph was never very well and later began having strokes. He wanted Esther— and only Esther— to take care of him, so Esther did her best to make candy and also to care for Ralph.

It seemed as though I'd have a lot of room on Fauver Avenue when I originally bought the house, but they made the streets narrow. When the people would come for their candy, I'd have to fix what they wanted. They'd start talking and visiting with me. Then somebody else would come—it was just like Grand Central Station. That would take too long, and the neighbors would get angry because the cars were blocking their driveways.

One day we got a letter from the City Building. The letter ordered "Mr. and Mrs. Price to meet at 2 o'clock in Courtroom #204 on the following Wednesday." I called and asked what the meeting was about, and the lady stated, "That will be discussed on Wednesday." Ralph and I were in a turmoil with days to wait. We were so upset that we could hardly eat, wondering what trouble we could be in. The hour of the meeting arrived. Our turn came. A lady called, "Mr. and Mrs. Price."

"We got a complaint from your next-door neighbor that your customers are blocking their driveway." I had been fearful of that because the builders were turning that rural area into a residential one really fast. The clerk said to me, "Why don't you buy on a nice wide street and build something where the parking won't bother anyone?" We were so relieved the situation wasn't any worse than that.

A few days later I came up Wayne Avenue and saw a realtor putting up a "FOR SALE" sign. I kept repeating the telephone number over and over until I reached home. I called and made an appointment to see it right away. The property seemed to be everything I needed—wide streets, one-hundred-foot frontage on a large piece of ground, and the seller was willing to accept a down payment that I could afford. I put fifty dollars down on it immediately. I signed for the property without getting in touch with Ralph for fear of losing it. They carried me for a long time until I could get a loan. (The owner had been stung by a bee and died instantly, and his wife and mother needed to live where they had care.) We got the deed for it in May of 1952. The house was one-hundred feet up a big hill. I thought I could come out in front of the house and build a front end onto it, but the hill was so steep, I was told I had to build on all or none of it. No builder could put a small enough building on that big hill for the money I could get. So there I was with the house but no way to make candy.

The back yard bordered on the cemetery fence. There was a gravel driveway at the rear of the house, but we had to go to the side street south of us and past another house. That house had a back porch with a swing. A lady sat there con-

"I saw this property at 1709 Wayne Avenue and visualized the future home of Esther Price Candies."

86

Open house of brand-new storeroom for Price Candies at 1709 Wayne Avenue, 1952.
Lady in apron in center is Ann Price.

Open house, 1952. Back row, left to right, Jack and Ann Price, Ralph and Esther, Eileen Price
Otto Kelley and William Otto. Front row, Linda Otto Lipsett and Bill Otto.

stantly with a gun and claimed she would shoot anyone that came in the driveway. Sometimes she was out in the yard and I would talk to her. One day she frantically called me and asked me to take her some place. She seemed hysterical and was having spasms. She directed me to her doctor's. He gave her shots and pills and calmed her down. After a few times I met her husband, and he said she was taking dope and thanked me for taking her to the doctor. I didn't see how anyone could live like she was—twisting, her eyes bulging, and her tongue seemingly too large for her mouth. About a month after that, her dad told me that she had such a bad attack that they had to put her in the state hospital. He told me he would have to sell the house as this had been going on for a long time, and he could no longer make the payments. I didn't have a dime, but I asked if I could buy it and make the monthly payments to him. It was only a short time until September when school would be starting and I should be making candy. He gave me the deed and I paid him a monthly payment. Because of the deed, I was able to borrow money to build a large kitchen on the rear of the house; I needed a big room where I could put my beater, cooker, and steel tables. With no basement and no bank to deal with, it was surprising how soon I had the cement blocks ordered to build a candy kitchen out the back door. They began digging the footers right away and added a cement-block room onto the back of the house. When we got the kitchen half finished, I had the mixer moved into it and made candy while the workers were finishing the room. Then I built a room out front facing Wayne Avenue that the customers could come in to buy candy.

I only had two big tables then: one I poured caramels on and one for marshmallow so I constantly was making candy. We ended up with seven tables. They were very heavy, and the water ran underneath them to cool the candy. My problem was that the water from the house ran over the furnace and was never cold enough. If the candy was not cooled enough, it would have a sugar center to it.

To dip chocolate, I bought a little ten-inch enrober (an enrober covers the candy with a curtain of chocolate and a belt carries it through a cold tunnel to set it so that the candy is able to be handled). It was seventy-five feet long. Later on, I got a forty-two-inch enrober that was several hundred feet long. Ralph thought I was crazy buying a machine that big, but right away I had to order another one so that we could make milk-chocolate candy on one and dark chocolate on the other. (From the very beginning we had some girls dipping all light and some dipping all dark. In southern Ohio, they preferred dark chocolate, and in northern Ohio, light.)

The enrober had a bottomer on it. The candy got coated on the bottom. It came out on a cold belt to set. Then it went through the curtain of chocolate, picked up more of a bottom and was coated with chocolate. There was a shaking device you could ad-

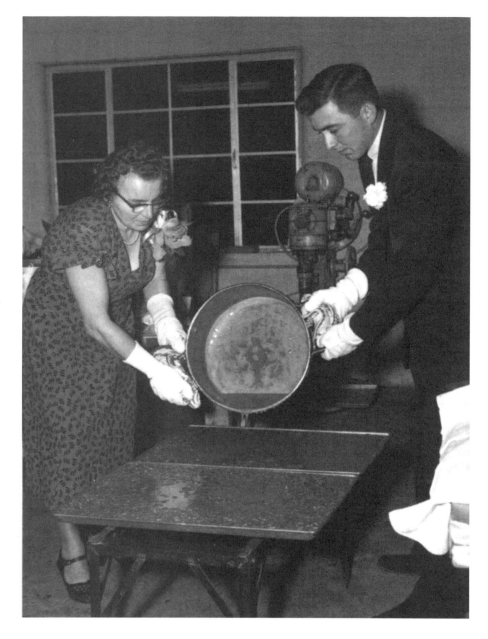

"Jack was always there when I needed him. He helped me in the business from the time he was eight years old."

just for the amount of chocolate you wanted. The machine also had a blower. I always liked a lot of chocolate on every piece so I didn't use the shaker. Then the candy came out on a long belt. At this point it was strung with an identifying design or covered with nuts. (The length of the belt is important because after the candy is dipped, it takes time until the chocolate is room temperature. The cooling tunnel gradually goes cold and then gradually reaches room temperature. The temperature is so critical on dipped chocolate.) Finally, the finished chocolates were packed in large cartons ready for the packing lines.

Until the very last years, we always dipped the cherries and peanut butter by hand. With the left hand, the dipper would shape the cherry and twirl it in the chocolate. As she set the cherry down, with the chocolate that remained on her finger, she slowly circled it on top making the recognizable O marking. When I started making caramel pecans, I only had a funnel full of boiled caramel, and I used a stopper for the caramel. We didn't have a caramel machine that you could pour the whole batch in until I could afford it.

"Two of my hand-dippers that were with me for many years. They're dipping creams and nut clusters."

I wasn't on Wayne Avenue more than one year when we went on a vacation, came home, and right in front of the store window, the city had put up a "NO PARKING" sign. I wanted to climb that pole and tear the sign down. Then I had to build onto the back end of the house. That's when I first built the hallway. The side of the house was already there. The people went around by the cemetery fence, parked in our back yard, and then walked through the back door and a hallway the length of the building to the salesroom. I had to make the hall presentable so I started buying gifts—pictures for the walls, crystal, and fancy figurines.

At that time we had to carry every piece of candy downstairs. Then Jack made a portable lift that I could set all the candy on and lower it. Then the candy was packed

"Ralph was my bookkeeper after he retired from Nabisco. Evelyn took over when Ralph's health failed."

downstairs. At first we only had three girls packing, and they had to pass each other to pack a whole box of candy. Then we had each of them pack only a part of the box. Much later, we packed the boxes on a conveyor. As the box passed, each girl would put in two pieces. When one layer was finished, a girl added a plastic liner so that the pieces on top

Sales girls at opening of Wayne Avenue store. Second from the right is Ann Price (Esther's daughter-in-law).

didn't ruin the ones below. At the end a girl would look at the box and add a dipped pecan, a dipped almond, or a dipped honeycomb chip to fill the box. Then she'd put the lid on, and it would travel on the conveyor to the wrapping machine—we wrapped every box in cellophane to keep the box airtight.

The first box I used to pack candy in was from the Piqua Paper Box Company. The inside of the box was brown and vanilla coated. The candy didn't taste like cardboard that way. I changed my wrapper according to the season. For Valentine's Day I had a paper with hearts on it. For Mother's Day I had some very lovely color like aqua. I was always getting books of foil paper and selecting one of the prettiest for my box cover. In the beginning I used red at Christmas; red and white for Valentine's Day tied in ribbon with hearts. So many people told me they were glad that I changed the color of the box with the season. That way they could get their wife, or their mother, candy for every occasion because it wasn't always looking the same.

I could never guess how many boxes I needed—I always had so many boxes left over and then would have to change boxes for another season. Many times I wouldn't change my boxes in time. I had so many boxes of odd colors around that I finally decided to use gold ones and only change the ribbon. Then I used red ribbon for Christmas, the heart for Valentine's Day.... The gold box was expensive looking; it always looked like a very good gift and saved me so much time and money.

Our own relatives lived in Cincinnati, and they were telling everybody about the candy. People were driving back-and-forth from Cincinnati to Dayton. I began hunting for a place for a store on a wide street in Cincinnati. Then I saw a "For Sale" sign on Reading Road, right across from a shopping center. There was a fur store next door. I felt it was a good location and bought it. Jack built a big concrete platform about eight-feet square and four-feet off the ground. He put a big copper kettle on it with a large wooden paddle inside it. Across the top we put spotlights and a big, arched sign PRICE'S CANDIES. [Later the name was changed to "Esther Price Candies" so as not to be con-

Montgomery Road store in Cincinnati.

fused with a midwestern company that called themselves "Price Candies."] Then Jack put a blower underneath the kettle which blew red plastic streamers to look like fire.

As in the past, parking soon became a real problem. I had to look for a place with more parking. Several years later I found property on Montgomery Road in Cincinnati. It had a nice parking lot with a long lane into it. There was a filling station across the street; on the opposite corner, a funeral home. The owner was selling tile out of the base-ment so I was able to get it zoned for business. There were two huge, beautiful trees that I couldn't bear to cut down—they were so beautiful and so old; yet I needed the space for parking. Then one day we had a storm. It lifted those trees right out of the ground and laid them down leaving two seven-foot holes. There was my parking.

Over the years I needed other locations for selling my candy. The people from Wright-Patterson Air Force Base were saying that it was too difficult to get across town after work, and they needed a place to pick up candy. Wright Field had many employees so I leased a building in a shopping center near it on Airway Road.

One day a man came into the Wayne Avenue store and said he didn't get off of work until 6 p.m., and by the time he got to the candy store, we were always closed. I asked him what place would be handy for him. He told me about the Kroger's Supermarket on North Main Street. They had just opened a gourmet section, where they only handled the finest foods. I went out there and talked to the manager. Many times other people had wanted to sell the candy, and I always refused because I wanted to keep my candy exclusive. This time I demanded my own refrigerated case with my name on it. The manager agreed. Later, most of the Kroger's started carrying Esther Price Candies.

It seemed as if I was always getting ready for a holiday. Valentine's Day followed Christmas, then Easter, then Mother's Day, then Father's Day, Sweetest Day.... Valentine's Day seemed to be the hardest of all because of all the hearts we had to fill, and we couldn't stack them because Valentine boxes had roses and flowers on top of them. Also, I packed them so full that the lid wouldn't fit down so that they *could* be stacked. With all my boxes of candy, I filled the box until it looked as if it couldn't hold another piece. The boxes always were overweight.

Valentine's Day was followed by Easter. Nobody knew how to shape the eggs but me. The cream was so soft that I had to toss the buttercream real fast in my hands and lay it down fast, or it would go through my fingers and not be the shape of an egg. Then every egg had to have enough room around it so we could decorate it. Ralph was such a good writer so he always wrote *Happy Easter* on each egg. The hole of the tube had

Esther's grandchildren, Easter, 1957. Back row, left to right, David Price, Karen Freese Brooks, Linda Otto Lipsett, Herb Freese, Bill Otto. Front row, Don Otto, Rick Price.

to be so tiny for him to squeeze the icing out of it. I made the icing, and it was so difficult to get it to just the right consistency without any lumps in it. Ralph would get so aggravated when it didn't come out of the tube just right. Besides *Happy Easter* and roses, I'd put a candy decoration on each one. The very first ones (when I was using the Shredded Wheat boxes for tables) were Snow White and the Seven Dwarfs. Later, I put a rabbit or something of the season on each egg. I didn't use chocolate molds until several years after I was on Wayne Avenue and had a cold room to set the chocolate instantly.

After Easter, there was Mother's Day. Years ago, Father's Day was not a big day. People gave cigarettes, but later they were trying to get Father to quit smoking. Father's Day grew to be very big at the candy store because they started giving him candy instead of cigarettes.

After summer vacation I always had to hurry to get ready for Sweetest Day in October. Then there was Thanksgiving Day and Christmas. We stopped taking mail orders before Thanksgiving Day because we couldn't make enough candy to fill them. I tried to talk people into giving candy for Thanksgiving and Christmas together. But it didn't work because the ones that bought candy for Thanksgiving ate it and came back for *more* candy for Christmas.

In December, the lines of customers were down the street, even around the corner. Some days were so cold that people were rubbing their hands and dancing around to keep warm until they could get into the store. Often they waited in line for at least an hour. It seems they didn't care if they had to wait all day—they wanted that candy. It made a nice gift for almost everybody. At first I said, "Only one box per customer," but

"In 1953, I started decorating the Wayne Avenue store for Christmas.
With Ralph and me are two of my grandchildren Bill and Linda Otto."

95

after waiting all that time, they were so angry that I decided to let them buy all they wanted until the candy ran out. It was just impossible for me to keep up with the demand.

Around holidays I worked every night until 2:30 or 3 o'clock in the morning. I hardly ever went to bed more than enough to lie down and get up again. At Christmas I'd work till I wouldn't have any strength left. I didn't even have strength enough to get up the stairs. I would have to sit on the bottom step and back up one step at a time.

What really urged me to build the big room connecting the two houses that I needed so much was so that we wouldn't have to walk across the yard in the night by ourselves. Ralph would go anytime he got finished carrying the day's money, and I would go up to the house hours later. One night, as I was gazing at the stars and counting my blessings, I heard the neighbor's collie barking. Then I heard someone rustling the leaves.

I rushed into the house and heard footsteps after me. I told Ralph that somebody was following me, that I had heard the dog barking and the leaves rustling. He got his revolver, loaded it, and put it on the nightstand where he could get it quickly. Nothing more happened that evening. Ralph said, "You really lost your senses getting that scared."

The next night I came across the yard by myself, even later than the night before. I didn't turn on any lights in the house. Ralph was already asleep. My side of the bed was next to the window. I sat on the edge of the bed—I was too tired to lie down. I heard somebody sliding against the side of the house and moving the screen from the bedroom window. I shook Ralph's foot and whispered, "They're here." Out of a sound sleep, he grabbed the gun and ran to the window. A bullet came through the window right above Ralph's head. He immediately dropped to his knees miss-

"The robbers were in the store while I was there. They came out the large side window of the candy kitchen just moments after I went home. I was thankful that I wasn't killed walking across the yard to the house. Within weeks I began building my candy factory connecting the two houses for Ralph's and my safety."

ing another bullet that would have hit him had he been standing. The burglars ran behind the big tree in the yard. As they ran, they kept shooting. The bullets went into the next room and lodged in the ceiling. Later when the police came, they said, "It's a good thing you didn't hit them because they were only trespassing." I realized then that we couldn't cross the yard anymore with the daily cash. I needed to connect the two houses so that we wouldn't have to go outside alone at night.

It was during the construction connecting the two houses that I had one of my worst disasters. Everyday I would put cement blocks up to the front door so that I could get in and out. The workmen would take them down to finish the porch. One morning a man came to finish buffing the floor in the new room. I had to let him in, but my cement blocks were gone again. I stood on top of blocks at the edge of the porch and thought I could jump. My heels caught in the hole of a block and turned me backwards onto the cement blocks that were laying down below. I got up and opened that door for him, and I started hurting so bad that I couldn't go on anymore. They said I'd better go to the hospital to get an x-ray. Somebody took me in the car. My back was broken in two places. The doctor wanted me to stay in the hospital, but I told him I just had to come home. I knew that I didn't dare let anybody know there was anything wrong with me— I had borrowed so much money, and they would all be wanting their money immediately if they thought I couldn't make candy. I got a bed that we could open up down in the candy store so I wouldn't have to walk far. I wouldn't take any pills for pain. I needed my full thinking power to make decisions. There were so many decisions to make in one

Connecting the two houses together and making the new, large candy store on Wayne Avenue, 1954.

day that I couldn't afford to be half asleep the way pills make me feel. It seems that I was in excruciating pain forever, but no matter how bad I felt, I never let it get in the way of making candy.

My shortest day was eighteen hours long. There were times in the early days that I worked around the clock, except for sleeping fifteen or twenty minutes. And I never sat down, except maybe to grab a bite of lunch. I seldom walked; I ran from the time I got out of bed in the morning until the wee hours of the next morning. After being on my feet on concrete floors so many hours, the veins in my legs would become ulcerated and infected. I was determined never to go to the hospital—my cousin's legs had not looked as bad as mine, and they had taken one leg off above the knee. After that happened to Mary Elizabeth, I wouldn't go to the hospital for any reason. Instead, I knew the healing power of chemicals in saltwater and believed if I could get my legs in the ocean, they would get better. On one occasion the fever in my legs was so great and the red streaks from infection had moved so fast that I phoned for tickets on the next plane to Florida. That same day Ralph and I flew to Florida. I went in the front door of the house, threw my luggage in the corner, got my swimsuit on, and went to the ocean. I sat for hours with my legs covered in sand and water. The pain was so intense that I had to sit up the first two nights, but by the third day, the pain, swelling, and redness miraculously went away. After a week we flew back to Dayton so I could make more candy.

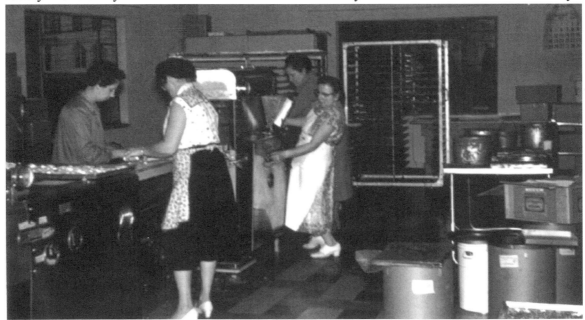

"The girls are placing the buttercreams on my first ten-inch enrober. I am at the far right in the long apron adjusting the belt. I had to carry the chocolate in kettles and dump it by hand into the hopper. The kettle of chocolate is on the right."

*"**I remember the first day that I went to work there**. It was on a Thursday, and I was sewing at home, and I thought, 'I bet that candy place hires people at Christmas time,' but I didn't think they'd keep them for more than a month or so. So I got up from my sewing machine and called Esther Price and she said to come on down at one o'clock. She asked me if I could play the piano and she held my hands that day and I just prayed they were cold because someone else had told me there were three requirements: you had to have cold hands, you didn't smoke, and you were able to type or play the piano. But having hot or cold hands does make a lot of difference. Did you ever get a box of candy and see the finger prints on it?*

"I was so surprised at her appearance—I thought that Esther Price probably wore a lot of make-up and real fancy jewelry and wouldn't get her hands dirty, and here she was working with everyone else. She usually wore cotton washable dresses rather than a real fancy something."

Helena Tartar and Johnnie Crutcher

Chapter Four

I think I lived on candy.

I couldn't use beet sugar. It doesn't dissolve right or make the candy smooth enough. I always used Franklin's extra-fine granulated cane sugar. Early on, I could buy fifty-pound bags, but when I began making larger batches of candy, I bought all of my sugar in one-hundred-pound bags to save money. I had a barrel with a lid on it aside my sugar barrel. In those days I lifted the hundred-pound bag onto that barrel with no problem at all. Then I would cut a corner off the bag and let the sugar drain into the barrel. (The first bags I used were made of cotton. Instead of cutting them open, I carefully removed the stitches, and Mama made tea towels out of everyone of them.)

Corn syrup was corn syrup, the only difference was, if you bought it from a grocery store, it was very thin. From the corn-syrup truck, it was thicker. Knowing how much to use just took practice. If I bought it from the factory, they delivered it and pumped it right into the tank underneath the candy pans where we melted the chocolate. Commercial corn syrup is so thick that you can twist your spoon in it, and when you lift your spoon out, the corn syrup stays on it.

For fudge, I used plain cocoa and sugar. I mixed the cocoa and sugar together. When I was in the country on vacation, Aunt Emmy used cream in everything, and it always made everything better so I always used cream when I had it and milk when I didn't. Later on, I added milk or cream, depending on what kind of fudge I wanted. I used cream when I wanted the fudge to stay softer. The fudge with milk had a firm base and I could cut it, but it would dry out more.

I added six heaping tablespoons of cocoa to three cups of sugar and then one cup of milk. When I first came home from school and made some fudge, I didn't have any corn syrup. In school we didn't have corn syrup at all. I knew that corn syrup would keep fudge from going to sugar, and I didn't want it to go to sugar. I added vanilla when the fudge was cooled and just ready to beat. You don't add vanilla when it's hot. I added butter, about an eighth of a pound for the three cups of sugar. I knew to add butter when my fudge was nearly finished. I took my fork and rubbed it all around the edge of the

Esther is dressed up for the candy-store open house. A customer once described her usual working attire in the following way: "There was a lady in a lovely pink smock with her hair fixed. She looked so nice, I thought that must be Esther Price. There was another lady at the rear of the store in an old house dress and an apron covered with chocolate. **That** *was Esther Price."*

"Easter trimmings on the Easter eggs the first Easter at the new candy store on Wayne Avenue, 1953. Finally I didn't have to carry the Easter eggs up and down two flights of steps. They sold so fast that I just kept making more and more. I never could make enough for the demand."

pan because as the candy was cooking it would splatter on the pan and that splatter would turn to sugar. The butter would get rid of all the crystals that might have formed so that the fudge didn't go to sugar.

I made white fudge mostly when I was out of cocoa. In fact, that's how I got started making white fudge—I was out of cocoa and I thought I'd make it without. It was so good that I kept on making it that way.

Every single thing I did was trial and error. If I didn't like it, I'd try it another way. When I'd go to the grocery store, I'd look for the different kinds of cocoa and vanilla, especially the different kinds of butter. I didn't like whipped butter as well as the good, old country butter. Whipped butter didn't go nearly as far—I only got about half when it was melted down. After we got into our house on Fauver Avenue, I started making my own butter. Jack and I went out to the farms looking for Guernsey cows. I had wide-mouth jars, and I could reach in them with my hand and scrape the cream out—it wouldn't pour out; it was too thick. That cream would only take a couple of turns, and it would be butter.

At home there was always the Watkins man that went door-to-door. He handled very exclusive things that we couldn't buy at a store. Watkins cinnamons and spices were so much better than what I could get on the grocery-store shelf. When I was making candy wholesale and had to make a lot of it, that little bottle of Watkins vanilla didn't go very far. I started buying vanilla by the quart. I wrote to the different companies that made extracts and asked for samples. I tried the samples in the candy. Some of them were as if I put nothing into the candy, and others added a good flavor.

In the early days Mama always had Hershey's cocoa and Walter Baker's on the shelf, as well as that Walter Baker's solid piece of chocolate that was called "Bittersweet." Mama baked, baked, baked all the time, and she made a lot of devils food cakes and things like that. I tried the two cocoas together and throughout my life kept trying anything that anybody told me about, or anything I saw new on the shelf. For awhile I used part of Hershey's and part of Walter Baker's cocoa, and I also used a little piece of Walter Baker's Bittersweet Chocolate. I didn't put the solid piece of chocolate in until the last five minutes, just so it melted; otherwise, it would go to the bottom and burn. Later, I discovered Nestles cocoa. I used it all by itself, and I loved the flavor of it. I used it from then on.

I let the fudge cook until it dripped slowly off the spoon in two beads; it was nearly finished then. When you tested it in cold water, if the water clouded up, it wasn't quite finished. When the water wasn't cloudy anymore, and it would form little balls, the candy was finished. I set the pan carefully on the cement someplace or in a pan of water to cool, and I didn't add the vanilla until I was ready to beat it. Fudge is supposed

"My eighth grandchild was born on Sweetest Day and named Candi Price. Her father (my son, Jack) is showing Candi how to place buttercreams onto the enrober."

"We were putting in a furnace on Fauver Avenue in 1950," Jack says. "One of the furnace men told me he knew where there was a Stanley Steamer. I left real early the next morning. The owner had died in 1922, and the Stanley was still sitting in the shed under a pile of straw. The lady (she was in her nineties and a real hermit) said she didn't think I'd want to give her what the car was worth. She said she had to get $70 for it. I told her I thought I could get that together."

"So early the next morning," Esther remembers, "he and Ann went to get the automobile. I couldn't wait to see the car. He pulled up with bushel baskets of parts and the wooden body of the Stanley Steamer. It looked like nothing to me. I wondered how he would ever get that put together. From then on every minute he had, he was sanding the spokes or something."

"I bought it in 1950," Jack continues, "and finished fully restoring it in 1957. That same year I built the all-glass showcase at the candy store on Wayne Avenue to house the Stanley Steamer. The car was in there from 1957 until the time the candy store was sold. At Christmastime a life-size Santa Claus was on the running board, and his arms would swing back and forth as if he was waving. One year I had two bicycles in the back seat. Another year the back seat was filled with boxes all wrapped up. We'd wrap all of the presents for the grandchildren early [at that time Ann Price was doing Esther's Christmas shopping] and we'd leave them in the back of the Stanley Steamer until Christmas. That car became a symbol of the candy store, and I started using the slogan, 'That old-time quality you'll remember.' "

A drawing of the Stanley Steamer appeared on Esther Price Candies
sacks for many years (see page 2).

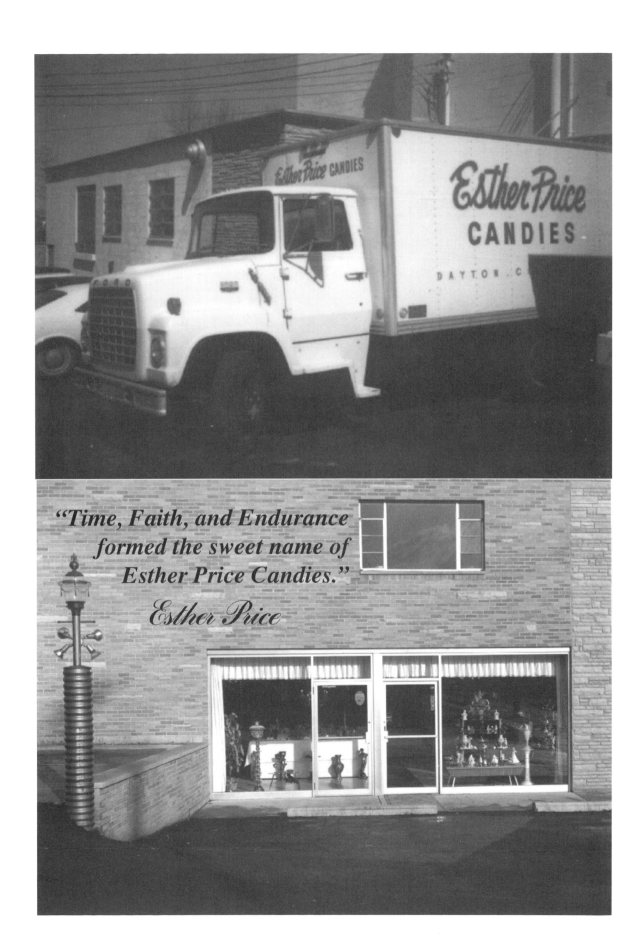

"Time, Faith, and Endurance formed the sweet name of Esther Price Candies."

Esther Price

to be stone cold to the back of the hand, but if I let it get that cold, my wrist wouldn't turn it so I beat it just before it cooled all the way.

I had to have a big iron table to pour the marshmallow on. A piece of marshmallow took up one corner of the candy box. It didn't weigh much at all, and everybody loved it. I could not sell marshmallow by the pound because we had to have one piece for each box. I could only make one kettle a day—that just about took care of the boxes we packed. I always got everything that I could ready the night before so I didn't waste a minute in the morning. I had two crocks and soaked the gelatin overnight in water. It would swell up twice the size. Then every morning I started making marshmallow as soon as I could get downstairs. I'd break all the eggs and then lift the yolks out with my fingers—I used twelve egg whites for each batch. I wanted the eggs to come from a bug-pickin' chicken that ran on the ground, and they had to be brown eggs—I always thought they were the best. I used Franklin extra-fine white sugar, corn syrup, and a little salt. Then I beat the egg whites until they stood in peaks. I poured the gelatin into the beater, then slowly dripped the syrup into the gelatin. Finally, I folded the egg whites in and added vanilla.

I would set the alarm for 4 a.m., and I was downstairs by twenty minutes after four. I don't know what I ate or what I put on. The main thing was that my employees came in at 8 a.m., and I had to be ready for every one of them. When I cooked candy in large kettles, it was impossible for me to pour the boiling syrup by myself. I had to have Jack help me. As soon as I moved to Wayne Avenue, I bought larger kettles and increased my production even further. I needed more help. I hired another man to work for me. He came in about 6 a.m. He had to have the candy cooked, poured out, and cooled to stone cold, then beat and ready for the dippers.

The chocolate had been put into the vat to melt the day before. The minute I got up, I would turn the chocolate melter on and stir the chocolate well; then I would stop it and add more chocolate because once I had melted chocolate in the vat, the next chocolate melted very easily. If I added too much chocolate at once, it would cool down too much so that it wouldn't melt. So I had a process of melting the chocolate, then stirring it and adding more, giving it a chance to melt. Those were ten-pound pieces. I finally got the chocolate in fifty-pound cases. I didn't have to unwrap every piece then. I would just throw them into the vat. Then I put on the pan of sugar for the marshmallow. It always helped to have the marshmallow finished and ready for the girls to dip in case the other candy wasn't completely ready.

I had the sugar weighed, the cream weighed, and the candy starting to stir by the time my assistant candymaker came in at 6 a.m. We had to keep a pan of chocolate in front of each of the dippers. About every hour we would add a little more warm chocolate. And I had to go around to the packing tables to see what pieces the packers needed; we were constantly changing our dipping girls onto pieces that we were out of so that we didn't have to stop our packing.

I think I lived on candy. I don't remember stopping very much and yet, in the early years I had to put on a meal for Ralph and the children. I would put on a pan of beans or spaghetti or something that would keep warm until Ralph got home from work.

I was thrilled through and through that I knew how to make candy. It seemed as though it was something given to me that I had to use. I just loved making the candy and seeing how it was going to turn out. I was thrilled every time I stirred a pan of candy.

After more than fifty years of candymaking, I sold the candy business and retired because of Ralph's illness. I still dream about making candy, though. In my dreams I am always working so hard high up in a building. I'm clearing out corners and setting up tables so that the girls can dip chocolates. I have the strongest urge to make another pan of fudge.

"Standing on this fence with Ralph in 1920, I never dreamed I'd be a candymaker."

"Not many years later, Ralph and I found it difficult to ever get away from our candy-making. We had very little time to relax."

Gone Fishing!

Esther

Four generations of Rohman/Price women: Linda, Esther, Eileen, and Ella, Dayton, Ohio, 1950.

About the Authors

Esther Price, the founder of Esther Price Candies, sold her candy business in 1976. During her candymaking years Esther received many honors, including one of the Ten Top Women of Dayton, Ohio, in 1975; a Kentucky Colonel in 1975; and the Junior Achievement "Spirit of American Heritage Award" in 1976.

Esther now lives with her daughter Eileen in Dayton. Esther was married to Ralph for nearly sixty years. She has three children, eight grandchildren, and nine great-grand-children.

Born and raised in Dayton, Ohio, Linda Otto Lipsett is the author of *Remember Me*, *To Love & To Cherish*, and *Pieced from Ellen's Quilt*. Linda is also a professional violist, who works in the motion picture, television, and recording industries in the Los Angeles area.

Linda (Eileen's daughter) is the granddaughter of Esther Price.

For additional titles write for our catalog.

Halstead & Meadows Publishing
P.O. Box 317211
Dayton, Ohio 45431